# Senior Moment

# Senior Moment

## Navigating *the* Challenges
*of* Caring for Mom

Monica Graham

NIMBUS
PUBLISHING
— NIMBUS.CA —

Nimbus Publishing Limited
3660 Strawberry Hill Street, Halifax, NS, B3K 5A9
(902) 455-4286 nimbus.ca

Printed and bound in Canada
NB1490

Editor: Angela Mombourquette
Cover design: Heather Bryan
Interior design: Rudi Tusek

Library and Archives Canada Cataloguing in Publication

Title: Senior moment : navigating the challenges of caring for Mom / Monica Graham.
Names: Graham, Monica, 1954- author.
Description: Includes bibliographical references.
Identifiers: Canadiana (print) 20200404164 | Canadiana (ebook) 20200404407 | ISBN 9781771089548 (softcover) ISBN 9781771085915 (EPUB)
Subjects: LCSH: Graham, Monica, 1954-—Family. | LCSH: Adult children of aging parents—Atlantic Provinces—Biography. | LCSH: Mothers and daughters—Atlantic Provinces—Biography. | LCSH: Aging parents—Care—Atlantic Provinces. | LCSH: Old age homes—Atlantic Provinces. | LCSH: Long-term care facilities—Atlantic Provinces. | LCGFT: Autobiographies.
Classification: LCC HQ1063.6.G73 2021 | DDC 306.874—dc23

Nimbus Publishing acknowledges the financial support for its publishing activities from the Government of Canada, the Canada Council for the Arts, and from the Province of Nova Scotia. We are pleased to work in partnership with the Province of Nova Scotia to develop and promote our creative industries for the benefit of all Nova Scotians.

# Contents

*Monica's mom at a family wedding in the early 2000s. "She's laughing at herself," says Monica, "because, as she will tell you: 'I am the funniest person I know.'" (Author's collection)*

## CHAPTER 1

# My Mother's House

~*~

*T*he last time I visited my mother at her house in Newfoundland, she cooked my favourite meal: roasted chicken breasts with vegetables.

But before we'd even had a chance to taste it, she shoved it into the garbage and offered me some homemade soup she'd found in her freezer. Then she confessed she'd smeared yellow dish detergent instead of vegetable oil over the skinless, boneless chicken breasts, and covered it with herbs and spices.

By the time she'd realized what happened, it was too late.

It was an easy mistake. Both the vegetable oil and the dish soap came in clear plastic bottles with yellow labels, and they sat side by side on her pantry counter. I could have done the same thing myself.

*Really, I could have*, I told myself. Except I never had. And as my visit with Mom progressed, I recognized this mix-up was typical of what her life had become in the few months since I'd last seen her.

She'd hidden her situation well, even from me—the person who telephoned her every day.

Twenty-five years earlier, just after she'd retired, I'd begun the daily practice of calling from my home in Nova Scotia at 7:30 A.M.—or 8:00 A.M. Newfoundland time.

Before that, I'd called less often, but always early, before I started work and when she was likely to be at home. If she didn't answer my early call or my subsequent calls throughout the morning, I told myself she was outdoors or couldn't hear the phone. But—what if? What if she'd fallen downstairs? Suffered a heart attack? What if she was lying there in pain, waiting for help?

Sometimes I'd call her neighbour, or my cousin, or my aunt, who would investigate and then report that she was weeding her garden in the pre-dawn darkness, that her phone was turned off, or that her radio was blaring so loudly it had drowned out the phone.

After a few such alarms, Mom and I made a pact that I, or someone designated by me, would call her every morning at the same time. If we didn't reach her, we would have reason to call for help—and possibly even call the police. The thought of police cars roaring up to her house with sirens screaming clinched the arrangement. Most mornings Mom pounced on the phone at the first ring. If she had to go somewhere early in the morning, if she had a hospital test or was travelling, she'd tell me the day before.

Over the ensuing 7,300 phone calls, give or take a few, I never picked up on how much both her memory and her physical strength were failing. She chatted easily about politics, religion, and people—just as she always had—so our conversations never yielded the critical information I gathered within the first thirty minutes of my visit to her home.

~⚹~

*When I'd arrived, my initial impression of Mom's house was that it was* the same as ever: a place that offered a comforting sense of welcome. There were no strange odours and there was no visible dirt. The cheerful decor included mementoes from ninety years of energetic living, with the kitchen table set, as usual, as if a dinner guest were expected any minute. That day the guest was me, but preparing the table for a surprise visitor was Mom's habit.

"I was taught to set the table as if Jesus was my guest," Mom had explained to me many years earlier, as she turned over a knife I'd just laid on the linen cloth. "The knife should face the other way." I doubt one's level of faith is indicated by the position of a knife on a table, and I still don't know the correct way to place cutlery. Although Mom's instructions were long wasted on me, she obviously still followed her own advice, right down to the cloth napkin (always cloth!) properly folded, usually in a napkin ring, and placed beside the fork.

The bare parts of the floor were clean and well swept. A small-ish fire glowed from the wood stove, just enough to be welcoming without being oppressively hot, and there were footstools and cushions for tired feet and backs.

It felt like home, almost—except my mother's current house had never been my home. Familiar, but not home. Mom had inherited it from her father more than forty years earlier. I had visited almost annually as a child, when it was my grandfather's house. Now it was Mom's.

Mom and I had not lived in the same house, or even in the same town, since my departure at seventeen for a summer job away

from the Cape Breton town we lived in at the time. That job was
followed by university and then by my marriage and settlement
in northern Nova Scotia.

Dad was an Anglican priest, and when he died eleven months
after I'd married and left home, Mom and my three teenaged
brothers were forced to move from the church-owned house that
had come with Dad's job. Although it was a traumatic experience
for all concerned, moving wasn't new to us. Throughout my childhood, our family had moved wherever Dad's work as a clergyman
took us. We had never lived long enough in any single house for
it to become a home—probably the reason that, as adults, we'd all
rooted ourselves deeply within the communities where we'd landed.

Throughout all the moves, Mom had developed a knack for
creating a sense of homecoming for us wherever she lived. She
managed just the right mixture of chaos and order where we didn't
mind leaving a half-read book on a chair. Our houses were always
clean enough—but not so clinical that wet boots couldn't be stood
behind the stove to dry.

Now, Mom's house seemed more or less the same as it had
always been, but after a while I began to notice that the cozy
kitchen was starting to look shabby, scarred, and spent—a bit like
the rest of the house, and a bit like its owner. Television handy-
man-comic Red Green could learn a thing or two from Mom, I
mused, looking around.

Mom had a set of Bass River arrow-back chairs, their significance impressed on us as children when we'd rocked backwards
on the rear legs. "All four legs on the floor!" Mom would snap at
us and, on occasion, at visiting bishops and other church brass. In
those cases, she'd add "sir" or "madam."

More than fifty years down the road the chairs still looked fine at first glance, but Mom wouldn't let me sit on them. "Here, you have this one," she ordered. She took the chair I'd chosen for herself, bracing her legs against the floor like a sailor on a tossing deck.

It took me a whole day to catch on to the chairs' general state of disrepair. She'd repaired the wobbly legs on three of the four kitchen chairs by wrapping the ends in Kleenex so they'd fit snugly into the holes on the seat-bottoms. She'd then tied the legs firmly together with used (but obviously still useful) shoelaces secured with fishing knots.

At that point, the wobbly chairs didn't matter much. I hadn't come to do a white-glove inspection; I'd come to Newfoundland to escort her back to Nova Scotia for her 90th birthday, where we would celebrate with family and friends from all over Canada. But I did take advantage of the next twenty-four hours to get better acquainted with my mother's house.

Mom had sensibly stacked her most-used items where she could find them when she needed them: favourite crockery on the lowest shelf in the wall cabinets; frying pan and pot on the stove; laundry detergent beside the little spin-washer; portable phone beside her chair; and, unfortunately, the dish detergent and the vegetable oil on the tiny countertop.

Her system worked most of the time. But if the phone rang while she was in the pantry, she forgot that it was beside the chair. She'd find it and answer just as her recorded voice began to ask the caller to leave a message, forcing her to search for the answering machine to switch it off.

If she emptied the jug of laundry detergent next to the washer, she'd buy another instead of opening one of the numerous backups she'd stored all over the house: in the porch, in the upstairs bathroom, and in the cupboard under the sink. The frying pan was easy to find, but during my visit she couldn't find the spatula to turn the breakfast eggs. I found it later, along with a slotted spoon, a ladle, and other utensils, stored in a plastic bag suspended from a hook in a corner of the pantry that extended deeply under the house's only staircase.

"How did they get there?" Mom asked in amazement.

"You must have had a reason to put them in the bag, Mom."

"Yes, I suppose I did, but I don't remember."

Out of sight, out of mind.

I am old enough to remember when plastic grocery and bread bags were novelties—treasures to be carefully saved and reused along with plastic margarine tubs and ice cream buckets. Eventually I learned to reduce, recycle, and reuse, but I swear Mom still had the first plastic bag Sobeys ever filled with groceries for her.

"You never know when someone is going to need a plastic bag," she told me more than once. Now, empty plastic grocery bags hung from the chair-backs; more bags oozed from the space between the fridge and the wall, and still others burst from the crevices between the armchair cushions. She had stashed bags inside cloth sleeves in the porch, the pantry, and the hallway. Loose bags occasionally floated across the floor like escaped jellyfish. These bags might hold nothing, or everything—including more bags, yesterday's mail, laundry she meant to hand-wash, or the aforementioned utensils.

She also saved everything plastic—just in case. If it was a plastic food container, she washed it and stacked it with all the others in the pantry, the storehouse shed, and in a corner of the bathroom.

"You never know when I might want it for leftovers [fishing bait/ paint/soaking paintbrushes/picking berries/bits of soap]."

She also saved anything that was, to her, unusual or potentially useful: the church bulletin from ten Christmases past, a forty-year-old pop-up birthday card, a tiny piece of driftwood in the shape (she said) of a walrus, a hundred straightened twist-ties saved in a rescued Styrofoam cup, bent rusty nails to be straightened and re-used, pens without ink and ink tubes without pens, decks of fifty-one cards—all of it, "Just in case. You never know."

Mom glued hunks of foam (saved, just in case!) to any corners where she might bump her head or her shins, and she stuffed drafty seams and cracks with crumpled newspaper and balled-up chicken wire. The wire kept out the mice, she explained. She covered the scars on the walls with art created by three generations of her descendants.

My brothers and I admired the independence and the ingenuity that prompted Mom to MacGyver her broken furniture together, to plant a vast vegetable garden into her 90th year, and to (sort of) maintain a car. I say "sort of" because her mechanic had refused to safety-inspect it just before my arrival that winter. When I got there she had been without a car for about two weeks, and she complained every day about the loss, not so much of her car, but of her independence.

"Take a cab," I suggested.

"Too expensive," she snapped.

"It costs less than buying a car and insurance and gas for the few times you'd use it," I argued.

"Well, maybe," she said, in a tone that made me fear she planned to just go out and buy a vehicle anyway. She was still an independent woman—albeit a forgetful and deaf one with woeful night vision.

～☙～

*Our admiration for Mom began to be tinged with concern for her safety* even before my brothers and I truly understood how dramatically her ability to care for herself had decreased.

The junk Mom saved was frustrating, but not dangerous. However, the potential for a house fire was frightening and had nothing to do with hoarding. We worried about the extension cords that connected the washer, fridge, radio, heater, microwave, toaster, kettle, coffee maker, and numerous other small appliances to the kitchen's two working wall outlets. To use one, something else had to be disconnected. Parts of the stove worked and other parts didn't. A stack of orphaned pot lids gave witness to the number of pot-bottoms burnt to destruction. We found the blackened and distorted pots in the storehouse after the snow melted—saved, no doubt, "just in case."

In my mind, I could hear Mom announcing: "Some day I'll need an old pot for something."

Later, an acquaintance described to my brother Dave how he'd observed smoke issuing from the back door one morning as he'd passed Mom's house. Knowing she lived alone, he pounded on the door, to no avail. He pushed his way in to find breakfast charred and smoking on the stove, and Mom in another part of the house, reading.

Fire was not our only fear. There was that incredibly steep staircase that brought to mind the family legend of an ancestor who'd fallen down a flight of stairs and died of a broken neck.

Mom had long refused my brother Howard's offer to install a ground-floor toilet, opting instead to chase up and down the stairs several times a day—or to pee into an ice cream bucket and empty it into the kitchen sink or out the back door—at least, that's what she hinted at. A practical solution, but more than a bit off-putting.

The stairs were no longer "up to code," warned a relative in the construction business. Mom counteracted our warnings about the steep, slippery stairs by having an extra railing installed—and by sticking duct tape to the soles of her slippers to increase their grip.

In her pantry, several food labels sported ten-year-old best-before dates. An under-the-kitchen-sink stockpile of undated homemade jams, jellies, and pickles included several jars with lids pinholed by rust.

A pretty old wooden rocker looked like a valuable antique, but I discovered that Mom had wrapped a sheet of corrugated cardboard in a pillowcase to cover the broken and missing rungs in the chair's back. A large cushion and a bright plaid blanket further disguised the repair. I envisioned the cardboard giving way and Mom getting stuck in the back of the chair, where she would have to wait until the next morning, after my phone call went unanswered, before she would be rescued.

Her flip-top pill organizer, with each day and hour marked in huge dark letters, sat empty on the windowsill. She dispensed her pills from an egg cup filled with multicoloured tablets and capsules. It was easier, she said.

"That one's for my blood pressure. No—it's this one. I forget what that one is for, but I have to take two a day...with food. Oh, I'd better take that one now. Don't let me forget that I already took it."

*Who reminds her when she's alone?* I wanted to know.

She scorned my suggestion that she ask the pharmacy to provide her drugs in convenient blister packs. "What? That costs more. I can take my own pills!"

Nope. She couldn't. Not all of them. Stray pills crunched underfoot, pulverised into the colourful braided rug that she and her equally eccentric cousin had proudly rescued from a ditch one summer. They'd stuffed it into Mom's little hatchback and dragged it home. It took them almost a week to assiduously clean and disinfect the rug, then they gave it a place of honour under the kitchen table.

"It's a perfectly good rug," Mom said. "Beautiful! I can't imagine why anyone would throw it out."

I could imagine all kinds of reasons, all the way from pet vomit to bloody murder and a wrapped-up body, but I said nothing.

The kitchen's corners held tippy stacks of newspapers and magazines, while balled-up tissues, illegibly scribbled notes, half-sucked candy, and other pocket detritus littered every surface. Strangely, given all the notes she'd written to herself, there wasn't a working pen or pencil in sight. She borrowed a pen from me to start a list of things to take with her to Nova Scotia.

~✧~

*After the detergent-chicken episode, I volunteered to cook meals while I was there, discovering in the process that her back teeth—her only teeth that weren't dentures—had deteriorated to the point where she couldn't chew meat unless it was stewed to a mush. Given that she was almost 90, the whole situation was to be expected, I supposed.*

I observed that Mom moved more slowly and carefully than she used to, and with less assurance. After a lifetime of tearing up and down stairs, over hills and rocks, and across meadows and beaches and city streets, she'd finally become cautious about tripping and falling.

Her clothing sagged noticeably from her shoulders, and she seemed, in general, a bit sad and tired. Even the laugh lines in her face drooped. Caring for herself and for her house had become too heavy a burden for her, I realized. It was time for her to be the cared-for, not the care-giver. But how could I make that happen?

This was not the first time I or my siblings had pondered this question during the twenty-five years since Mom had retired. More than a decade before her 90th birthday, my husband and I had offered to build an attached suite at our home where Mom could live for the winter. We theorized that she could return each spring to her father's beloved century-old house in Newfoundland and come back to us when it got cold and the snow got deep. She would remain independent as long as possible, with us nearby.

We thought the plan might help her ease gradually into a new living arrangement when the time came that she needed daily assistance. By that time, we speculated, she would have established friendships in Nova Scotia, gotten used to a different church and new seniors' groups, and could stay longer in her own home—the one that was attached to our place.

But she would have none of it. And while we were disappointed we'd have to come up with a Plan B, and maybe a Plan C and D, we certainly understood her stubborn independence.

After all, it had been bred into all of her children.

*Mom as a young woman, hand-washing laundry during a camping trip in Saskatchewan, 1947. (Author's collection)*

## CHAPTER 2

# A Life Well Lived

***~❖~***

**M**om had always been a poster child for independent living.

After Dad died, she'd looked after my brothers until they were all grown and flown. She'd held responsible jobs in the education sector, travelled all over Canada and beyond, and was involved in her church and in several volunteer organizations. She'd earned a good salary and answered to no one. More importantly, she'd remained vigorously healthy, with a strong personality that demanded room for expression. Her family gave her that space, having been raised to expect the same freedom from family restraints that she had always enjoyed.

Mom and Dad both encouraged early independence in their offspring; they had both left home to make their way in the world when they were just teenagers. Mom was barely seventeen when she left the then–British colony of Newfoundland for Canada on September 3, 1945, the day after the Japanese surrender ended the Second World War. She had been out of high school for a year at that point, working for a local merchant, and felt ready to spread her wings. She intended to travel to Montreal to study nursing at the same hospital where her older sister had trained.

She took the ferry to the mainland, and as she went through customs at North Sydney, she wondered if leaving Newfoundland had been a mistake. She had to wait in line in a "chicken cage"— behind the wire poultry netting used for decades at Canadian points of entry to delineate the humiliated "them" from the proud "us."

The customs agent asked for her destination. She said she was going to stay with relatives in Verdun and go to school. "Verdun is a suburb of Montreal," she added, in case he was about to ask.

"I know where Verdun is," he sneered. "You could fit twenty of your little Newfoundland town into Verdun."

She held her tongue about Corner Brook being a full-fledged city, much bigger than North Sydney. She fired him her haughty look—a look that could kill at twenty paces, as all her children knew.

On the wharf, she found dilapidated taxis lined up, their ragamuffin drivers screaming "Wanna taxi, lady? Wanna taxi?" Thankfully, she was travelling with a companion whose cousin was meeting them. They would stay overnight in Cape Breton and leave on the morning train for Montreal.

There was a dance in the town that evening, and Mom was persuaded to attend. She didn't enjoy the drunken men and women, the loud conversations, or the fist fight that eventually broke out.

*The mainland is terrible*, she thought, ignoring the fact that Cape Breton is an island. *Maybe I should go back home to Newfoundland.*

But she wasn't about to give up just two days away from home, so she carried on.

~*~

*After she arrived in Montreal, Mom was dismayed to learn that her grade-eleven marks weren't good enough to get her into nursing school, despite the fact that she had repeated her final year of high school in an attempt to achieve a higher average.*

Her father, my Gramps, had supplied her with enough emergency money to get home to Newfoundland if she needed to, but her pride wouldn't allow her to run back with her tail between her legs—as she put it when she recounted the story. She needed a job, as did the scores of other immigrants from Newfoundland and the multitudes of soldiers returning from the war.

She eventually found a job inserting stiffening into dress and shirt collars at a garment factory in Montreal's east end. The work was easy enough, but she was the only English-speaking person in her shop and she hated the repetitive assembly-line process. She lasted three days and then walked out, leaving her pay behind. The relocated Newfoundlanders who'd helped her find the job, and with whom she boarded, disapproved heartily, but Mom soon found another—better—job. A well-to-do Westmount family hired her as a governess to care for four rambunctious little boys.

"It was almost like being a nurse," she said seventy years later, admitting that the position satisfied a yearning for authority and respect. "I had a white uniform and white shoes. I looked after people." And with that, her wish to become a registered nurse evaporated.

Mom's cousin and best friend, Nellie, soon joined the same Westmount household as a maid, on Mom's recommendation. (This was the same woman who would help her save the braided rug from the Newfoundland ditch many decades later.) Mom's tales of their escapades were my favourite bedtime stories as a child, and I looked forward to the day when I could leave home for similar adventures—although I'm not sure that was Mom's intention in telling those tales!

Mom and Nellie were eventually separated when their employers moved to a mining community in northern Quebec and could take just one servant. They took Mom, and found a wealthy relative who was delighted to hire Nellie. Throughout her working life, Nellie was a much-sought-after housekeeper for wealthy Montreal-area families, among them a member of the British royal family who kept a pied-à-terre in the city. Mom, on the other hand, spent most of her adult life in one or another of Canada's most isolated communities.

Upon their arrival in northern Quebec, Mom's employers encouraged her to attend high school in their new community. She did, and also became a loyal member of the local Anglican church's youth group. Through that group, she discovered that women could study theology and find work within the church. For her, it was a dream come true. Her employers, though, wept when she graduated and decided to apply to the Anglican Women's Training College in Toronto to train as a missionary.

It was no surprise to her family back in Newfoundland. As a child, Mom had been fascinated by church. While other little girls played with dolls, Mom stood at her baby sister's high chair, enthusiastically pounding the tray as she delivered sermons to the dolls—and to any family members or friends who succumbed to her entreaties to join the congregation.

Besides Nellie, Mom's other best childhood friend had been the minister's daughter, Jane. They spent a lot of time at each other's homes, which allowed Mom to observe the clergy household's preparations for weddings, funerals, and big events in the church year. If the church had accepted women for ordination in those days, Mom might have applied to divinity school, but in the late 1940s it wasn't an option. Now, though, she could be a missionary.

❧

*Once ensconced at the women's college Mom talked her way into divinity* classes at the all-male Trinity College, the training ground for High Church Anglican clergy. It was here that she met the man who would later become my father.

At the end of her second year, five years after leaving Newfoundland, Mom returned for a two-week visit with her parents. When she went back to Canada—which Newfoundland had recently joined—it was to work with the church's Sunday School by Post program, delivering scripture and theology to isolated farm families on the Canadian Prairies. Mom and my future father carried on their romance by mail the whole time. She travelled west by train on hard wooden seats meant for both sitting and sleeping during the three-day journey. Passengers brought food to cook on a stove at the back of the railcar—and when Mom ate through the small picnic she'd brought with her, her fellow travellers shared their larders.

"The people on the Prairies were some of the finest people I ever met," she declared sixty years later. "They were so generous and kind; not a mean one amongst them."

She travelled by van all over the plains that summer, in dust storms and gumbo mud, camping out near wild bulls and dynamite stockpiles, meeting bush pilots and bona fide cowboys. When that stint was over, Mom stayed in the west. She served for three years with the Bishop's Messengers, a group of female missionaries who, clad in navy and white uniform dresses, ran church outposts in isolated Manitoba communities.

At the end of her three years on the Prairies, she went home to Newfoundland to marry Dad, who had been appointed to a church in a fishing village on the east coast of Newfoundland. Their first home, a rambling old house with inadequate heat and carry-the-bucket–style plumbing, was a two-day "Newfie Bullet Train" ride (as they called the passenger train that had been sarcastically named for its slow pace) from Mom's parents' place. In good weather it was almost a week's journey from Dad's parents' place in Montreal.

After deciding that four years was the optimum length of time to live in any one place, they moved to the Prairies, then to Quebec's North Shore (also known as Quebec Labrador), to the Gaspésie, and to Cape Breton. Over those years Mom's mother died, Dad's father died, and they had four children within the first six years of their marriage.

When Dad died unexpectedly in 1973 in Cape Breton, Mom didn't return to Newfoundland. Despite the fact that Gramps, Mom's three siblings and her siblings' families lived in Newfoundland, and two of my brothers and I attended university in the Maritimes, Mom packed up and took my youngest brother off to Quebec. She'd been offered a job there teaching life skills to adults. While she was there, she rediscovered her love of skiing and learned to play golf, which she subsequently taught her children—and grandchildren, too, as soon as they could stand up and hold a club.

Her job gave her the summers off, so she decided to check a lifelong goal off her list: to drive across Canada. With a girlfriend to help with the driving and her nine-year-old godson in the back seat, she filled her little car with camping gear, made a list of friends to visit—and drove to the Pacific Ocean.

After that, with Canada in her rear-view mirror, she began to talk about visiting England—but that would have to wait a while.

~·~

*Over the next several years, Mom's father died, Dad's mother died, and I* gave birth to three children. All of Mom's children soon followed my lead, settling with families into jobs and homes wherever we happened to land. None of us had grown up with an allegiance to any special place, so we created our own "homes and native lands."

Mom finally returned to Newfoundland when her Quebec position ended and she had no further prospects there, given that she was unable to speak French. She moved into the house her father had bequeathed her, and which she had rented to a sequence of family members until that point. Within a few months she found a job at the junior college in Corner Brook that required her to live on-site, so she rented out the house again.

She was employed as housemother in a coed residence, a position she held until her retirement fifteen years later. During that time, she established stronger bonds with her brother and three sisters and their families who lived in the area. She formed deep friendships with her skiing, fishing, golf, and hiking buddies, became ensconced in the local social scene of dinners, church, and

CNIB and VON meetings, and informally adopted many of the students she tucked under her wing. They became temporary family members, visiting Mom at her home, writing letters to her, sending wedding invitations and baby pictures, and generally staying in touch over the years.

This job also gave Mom the summers off, since the students were not in residence. She divided her time among her grown children and their families, travelling to our homes all across the country.

She finally got that visit to England when Jessie, a friend who'd emigrated to Canada as a war bride, wanted her company at the celebration of the 40th anniversary of D-Day. By all accounts, the two widows had a wild time touring Britain before boarding the ferry to cross the English Channel to France.

It was well after midnight when they arrived in a French port, the name of which Mom never could remember. It was dark. Mom and Jessie didn't speak enough French between them to order a sandwich, never mind to arrange transport to the various locations involved in the D-Day ceremonies. They wandered around the terminal until the cleaning staff became concerned and introduced them to a fellow who happened to be a British news reporter. He assumed the role of their guardian, driving them to the D-Day celebrations and to the cemetery where Jessie's Canadian soldier husband was buried. The journalist also interviewed them along the way, and the escapades of these two old Canadian widows became part of the international news coverage of the D-Day anniversary.

My husband and I took our children from northern Nova Scotia to Newfoundland so we could be there to visit with Mom when she returned. However, Jessie died suddenly upon her arrival back in Canada, and Mom, heartbroken, stayed with Jessie's family in New Brunswick until after the funeral.

When Mom retired, she moved from her college digs back into Gramps's house (as we called it). She had come full circle. Finally, she was home; she had a place of her own and she didn't want to leave, except to take two or three trips a year "upalong" or "'cross the island" to see her children, grandchildren and, eventually, her great-grandchildren.

~·~

*Ten years after Mom's retirement, she won a role on a "living history"* reality television show called *Quest for the Sea* that was to be filmed that year in an abandoned outport on Newfoundland's east coast.

It was Mom's chance to be a performer at long last. She had always loved cheering people up and playing the fool, whether on a stage or in daily life. She'd acted in hundreds of skits for fundraising concerts and had often served as Master of Ceremonies at events, where she'd assigned me to find clean jokes for her to tell while actors changed scenes and costumes.

In their younger days, she and Nellie had even developed a routine they'd perform when they visited The Home where Mom now lives. Mom would play Queen Elizabeth, and Nellie, much taller, would play Prince Philip. They'd make a brief appearance as the aging Royals and then duck out to change back to their ordinary selves. "You missed the Queen!" the residents would exclaim when Mom and Nellie returned. Mom and Nellie never gave away their alter egos.

Although Mom had a lot of fun with these amateur theatrics, she always regretted never making it to the "big screen." So when the 2002 search began for Newfoundlanders willing to participate in a re-creation of 1937 outport life—to be televised in 2004—Mom was on it. She visited us in Nova Scotia to get help with the application. My daughter chased her around with a video camera, recording Mom skiing, walking though the woods, and sitting in a chair talking to the camera. Even though she used her "preachy" voice for the video, she got the part.

I'd watched other shows in the series and had misgivings about Mom's participation. The programs featured groups of strangers living together as Prairie pioneers, tackling the Chilkoot Pass on their way to the Klondike, and paddling to Hudson's Bay. Although touted as historical re-creations, they were essentially reality shows aimed at showcasing human interactions in difficult situations.

There was no script, just a situation to get through with people you probably wouldn't choose as teammates if you had a choice. Nice enough people, but unpredictable strangers. Mom couldn't be persuaded to watch an episode.

"Oh, stop worrying. It will be fine. I can get along with anyone. Nothing bad will happen."

Famous last words.

She spent the whole summer of 2003 with nine strangers on an island in Placentia Bay, being followed around by film crews as they simulated life in 1937 with no electricity, no food except what they could raise or catch or find, a cranky wood stove for cooking, and an outdoor toilet. Such privations didn't bother Mom, having lived through all these conditions in real life, but she complained about the props—specifically the wood stove, a prop from another television show—and she protested the assumptions upon which the show was based.

"I remember 1937," she said, listing a legion of historical inaccuracies in the production. "We had food and fish and vegetables and berries left over from the previous year. We weren't starving like they had us doing. The men cut firewood all winter. They brought in dry wood every day all year long, by God, if they wanted a cooked meal."

She was disappointed with the format, as I'd expected. With no script, the cameras followed the cast around through good and bad.

"After a while we didn't notice them," Mom said later—which explained why the camera was able to catch her just being herself.

The production company stitched together a good four-part series, but Mom didn't want to watch it. She'd developed a strong dislike for a couple of other cast members, and could barely speak to them or look at them by summer's end. She returned home thinner and quieter than I'd ever seen her. In bits and pieces she divulged the circumstances that contributed to her unhappiness, including the lack of food, the encouragement by the producers of personality conflicts, and the lack of country-life skills among the cast.

While she would not admit that the show had taken a physical or emotional toll, it was obvious to everyone else that the experience had left a bitter taste in her mouth. It marked the end of Mom's yearning for a stage career, and the moment she lost the sense of adventure and naïveté that had allowed her to go through life expecting everyone to like her.

Ten years after she'd retired, that summer made Mom old. After that, she stayed closer to home, travelling less often. She gave up some of her volunteer work and spent more time with family and close friends.

~•~

*Mom's twenty-five-year post-retirement sojourn at Gramps's house* represents the longest period of time she ever stayed in one place. None of her children live near her and we have not lived together in one house, or even in one community, for almost fifty years.

Though we are alike in many ways, my brothers and I have different lifestyles, different expectations of our lives and our children, and different plans for our futures. In light of Mom's continuing declarations of independence, we couldn't, and didn't, wait for Mom to decide her future so we could plan ours.

She remains our common point of reference, though. We talk about her, we worry about her, we share our individual news about her. Until recently, she was the clearing house for all family news: we'd tell Mom and she would share it with everyone else. But except for considerations like vacations, visits, family celebrations and events, or regular phone calls, our life plans have not included her for decades.

In our absence, Mom had no qualms about asking favours of relatives, friends, or neighbours. They took her to appointments, shovelled her driveway, and fixed her appliances without reward. From our perspective, it didn't seem fair that they should assume responsibility for her, even though they swore they didn't mind, and Mom swore she was happy with the arrangement.

We knew Mom's life would be difficult without them, and as we often would in the months to come, we felt both guilty and grateful.

## Chapter 3

# The Time Is Coming

~❖~

*L*uckily for all of us, Nellie retired from her work in Montreal around the time of Mom's film experience and began spending her summers with Mom in Newfoundland. She was with us all when we celebrated Mom's 80th birthday in 2008. We rented a hall and hired the church ladies to cater the party, which was followed by a raucous Christmas-in-July celebration at Mom's.

Looking back, it feels like the last time Mom was her "normal" self was at her 80th birthday party. Soon after, she began to pick on particular relatives or neighbours, who could do nothing right in her eyes. She shunned them in public, called them names behind their backs, and complained unceasingly about their failings, which were visible only to her.

This was profoundly worse than the lifelong habit she'd had of passing judgment on people. I remember as a child hearing her begin many sentences with the words, "The trouble with [insert name] is...." They didn't listen, they weren't educated, they weren't raised well, they were proud or stupid, they hadn't been outside their neighbourhood in their entire life—and so on. There was a litany of troubles that could affect a person's behaviour, in Mom's opinion. Her children grew up following her example; we were quick to our conclusions, too! Life eventually knocked the habit out of us, but Mom kept on, oblivious, until she reached the point where she could no longer remember the reasons for her aversions to certain people. Her once-calm analyses became vicious condemnations.

The habit had exacerbated a rift at her church. The details are unclear, and it eventually healed, but it left more scars. Mom no longer enjoyed worship leadership as she once had. She'd begun in her teens, and was possibly the longest-serving Anglican lay reader (or licensed lay minister) in Canada. At one point we tried to get national recognition for her service, but though she was thankful that we'd noticed the achievement, Mom never gathered the documents for us to submit. We weren't sure if she was being deliberately uncooperative, or if she just couldn't recall where she'd put them. We let it go.

Mom's next milestone birthday, her 85th, was marked by a year-long stream of visitors. Although her birthday was the first time I'd been in her house for five years, I'd seen her a few times a year and had spoken with her on the phone every day. Up to that point, I hadn't noticed anything more concerning about her behaviour than the fact that she sometimes repeated stories.

But on this occasion, I remember exchanging wide-eyed glances with my brother Dave's wife, Polly, over Mom's strange behaviour. We all noted the disorganized storage, her task-related confusion, her memory loss, and her new willingness to sit and be waited on. Later during that visit, Mom privately told me that she worried that mini-strokes might have affected her memory, although no such thing showed up during a subsequent medical exam.

"Mom, why don't you get someone to help you around the house?" each of us asked, in one way or another, and got the same answer: "No."

Without a professional recommendation that Mom needed help around the house, and because she had no worrisome medical issues at all, there was no persuading her to accept assistance.

At this point Mom would often visit her children and their families, flitting from offspring to offspring, but she would get bored or annoyed after a week or two. Then she would announce she was going get the bus in the morning to move on—either to the next child's home, or back to her own. After she left we always waited nervously to hear whether she'd reached her destination. It was at least a two-day trip from my home to hers, involving a bus trip, an overnight ferry crossing, and another bus trip on the other side. After much persuasion, Mom had agreed that trips to the mainland should be punctuated with at least one overnight stay with my brother Howard in Halifax or with me, whatever her destination. She consistently refused our offers to drive her to the ferry or to book a flight for her to or from Newfoundland. For some reason she refused to fly, even though our family had happily flown in tiny bush planes all over northern Quebec and Labrador many years earlier. Not for Mom, any more. She never had any qualms, though, about sailing across the Gulf of St. Lawrence at night, in a gale, in any season. Each time she arrived she would declare that the sea had been as "smooth as a millpond—not even a ripple."

Around the time Mom had turned 80, she'd begun asking me to book her ferry reservations. I'd tell the company representative that she was elderly, determined to travel independently, and that I'd appreciate it if the stewards could keep an eye on her. They did, tactfully, never tipping Mom off that she was receiving any kind of special treatment. I didn't tell Mom either. The ferry company never billed me for their attention to her, but it would have been worth it for the peace of mind. The effort paid off for them, too: they couldn't buy the kind of good public relations Mom gave them. She praised the crew, from the stoker to the captain, for their welcoming attitude and kind assistance. She told everyone to take the Marine Atlantic ferry—"as good as a cruise," she said. "Better."

Not that she'd ever been on a cruise.

~*~

*Despite our precautions, we knew that anything could happen on one of* those ferry trips, and especially to Mom. She'd been aboard the ship during fires and hurricanes, and had been storm-stayed at the terminal more than once. We'd known her to get off the bus at the wrong stop.

On one occasion she got a ticket from the ferry terminal to the Halifax airport, where my brother was to meet her. She got off at the departures terminal instead of at the bus stop, where Howard had parked to wait. The bus came and left with no sign of Mom. Maybe he'd mistaken the time? He checked—no, he had it right. Friends and family were dispatched to chase the bus up the highway to the next stops. Howard called the bus company, to no avail. He was a nanosecond from dialling 911 when his cellphone rang.

It was Mom, who had borrowed a cellphone from a stranger in the airport terminal.

"He looked like a Newfoundlander, so I asked him," she explained when Howard finally found her. "He really was a Newfoundlander, too. 'Of course, my dear,' he said to me, and he even dialled the number."

Mom swore she hadn't gotten off at the wrong place, and that the mix-up was all Howard's fault for waiting at the wrong stop!

Crossing the Cabot Strait on another occasion, Mom had befriended a Swedish university student who was trying to see Canada from east to west on a shoestring budget. She promised him that my husband and I would show him our part of Nova Scotia before he took his next ferry to Prince Edward Island. We did, because we are as bad (or as good, depending on one's perspective) as Mom about offering rides, meals, and beds for the night, and we enjoy showing off our country. To this point, all our unexpected guests have been lovely, but it wouldn't be out of the realm of possibility for Mom to generously pick up an axe murderer.

~✲~

*A year or two after Mom's 85th birthday, she suddenly announced that someday, when she got old, she wanted to move to Nova Scotia.* Howard and I live in Nova Scotia, and the rest of our family, which by then was spread from eastern Newfoundland to the Yukon, could just as easily visit her in Nova Scotia as in Newfoundland—perhaps more easily.

"Maybe you could look around and find me a little apartment, just for this winter," she suggested to me.

I promised to look, and soon found one that almost met her requirements. The ground-floor apartment was inexpensive, it was about fifteen minutes from my home, and it was in the same village where we attend church. The landlord, a cheerful fellow who had made a late-in-life career of helping seniors and teenagers, had met Mom previously and was happy to offer the place to her. The village has a library, basic shopping, and a whirlwind of church and community activities. The only drawback was the apartment's size.

"Oh, three bedrooms! Way too big," Mom said.

"You would have room for people to visit you," I countered. "Someone could even stay all winter. What fun you'd have."

"Yeah, but...," and she began a litany of reasons she didn't want to move. She'd have to heat a second home; she'd have to keep her car going; she'd have to clean her apartment all the time and then return home to clean her house; she'd have to buy groceries and cook them; she'd just get into activities and it would be time to go back to Newfoundland; it was too far from Newfoundland—and on it went.

She'd never really intended to move, I realized.

"No, when I move, I'm not going to cook any more. I'm finished fudging for myself," she announced.

Had I heard correctly? I paused, thinking fast about how to nail down that statement. "You mean you'd prefer some kind of residence or home," I said.

"Oh!" she sounded as surprised as I was. "Yes, I suppose that's what I want."

"I think that's a great idea, Mom," I said. "I'll look around and see what I can find."

Did I get off the phone and do a happy dance, complete with fist-pumps? I sure did! Unfortunately, my reaction was premature.

As the years passed, Mom continued to refuse to move. She also met with derision any suggestion that she hire someone to help with heavy housework and some of the cooking. "Heavy housework? What heavy housework? I don't get my place dirty. And I can cook. No! I don't want anyone coming in here."

There was one possible exception. If one of her (by then) middle-aged children was willing to leave their job, spouse, children, and grandchildren to move in with her, she'd accept their help. That would be just fine.

We wouldn't, and we didn't, for many of the same reasons she refused to live with us. We were all independent and we had our own lives to live. Also—truthfully, and not-so-secretly—we all dreaded the idea of having to live with her for any great length of time. She would argue at the drop of a hat and she had no hesitation about telling anyone how to do anything at all—a trait that frequently led to confrontations. She slammed dishes and banged doors and dragged furniture around with abandon.

As she aged, her habit of choosing a person upon whom she would vent her anger and frustration made her visits a special kind of hell. Some friends and family members came to dread her visits. They loved her, but they wanted to feel loved in return. The message they got from Mom, rightly or wrongly, was total disapproval and disdain.

We wondered if her worsening behaviour represented the beginnings of dementia, but this suspicion remained unconfirmed. Noticing and wondering didn't make life with Mom any easier.

Despite all that, I felt guilty about not picking her up, lock, stock, and barrel—against her will—and bringing her to live in our house.

"Don't do it," one person after another told me. "You can't do it."

Logically, when I was cool-headed enough to clearly consider the situation, I knew I couldn't. Emotionally, though, I wanted to. After all, my cousin Marg had brought her aged and widowed mother—my mother's sister and my aunt—to live with her until her death. Marg's mother had brought her father, Gramps, to live with her and her family until he passed. Gramps had dementia, and Marg's mom was disabled and on oxygen, so it wasn't easy for their caregivers. But they did it.

I couldn't. I struggled, and still do, with being less kind and generous than both my aunt and my cousin. I had to come to terms with the fact that my mother and I don't know each other as well as my aunt and my cousin knew each other. I have lived more than three-quarters of my life away from the rest of my family—not yet as many years as Mom had lived away from her father and siblings. Why should I feel guilty when she'd never appeared to?

The family joined forces to help her begin to plan a move—somewhere. We toured her around nursing homes and assisted-living residences whenever she visited Nova Scotia. She liked a couple.

"Get my name on the list," Mom said a few times over five years.

~ * ~

*So we began tackling the logistics of moving Mom from Newfoundland to Nova Scotia in earnest.* One possible drawback was that she would have to live in Nova Scotia for three months before becoming eligible for medical care (and thus, for provincially-supported housing). In those three months, she would have to be self-supporting, meaning that she would have to either live with one of us, live in an unfamiliar apartment, or pay out-of-pocket to live in a private seniors' facility.

By that point, we all knew living with us was a no-go except in an emergency. She could have stayed with any one of us for a short time, but financial circumstances, commitments to other family members in more immediate need, job requirements, and personal health issues meant that none of us had the time or resources to provide long-term care that was any safer or happier than Mom's current situation. In her own home, Mom knew the location of the bathroom, the phone, the locks, the teapot, and everything else. Left alone in one of our houses for even an hour, we feared what could happen. She could torch the kitchen trying to make coffee on a stove she didn't know how to use, lock herself outdoors in her pyjamas in -20°C, or fall down the stairs trying to do us a favour by cleaning them.

All of these things were possible, as we'd discovered to our dismay. We'd caught her trying to cook on the stovetop with a plastic pot, getting entrances and exits confused with interior doorways, and stumbling over non-existent obstacles. I couldn't bear to think about having to follow Mom around every minute. No doubt she would hate it, too!

The second possibility—having Mom move from her house to live independently in strange quarters closer to one of us—was worse than the first option. There would be no one at all to keep a watchful eye on her.

We realized that, wherever she went, she would need guidance through her settling-in phase and someone to keep a steady watch on her afterward. That meant the best option would be some kind of assisted-living arrangement that would match Mom's needs and wants, as well as her finances. We weren't sure whether such a place existed.

Also—we had almost no idea what her financial situation actually was. Several times I tried to ask Mom, diplomatically, what she could afford. "Oh, I've got enough," was her invariable answer.

Mom always had money when we were with her. She flashed around $50 and $100 bills when we took her shopping, but she squeezed pennies so hard they moaned.

So without knowing exactly how much money she had, I researched housing options for her. A Nova Scotia official offered to work with her Newfoundland counterparts to seek a solution, and I agreed. Things were looking up! I suggested to Mom that she visit us for a while so she would be present for any interviews that arose. Any excuse for a trip to Nova Scotia: she was at my place within a few days.

A few days later, after visiting some local homes for special care, Mom sat at my kitchen table and declared that she'd decided to live out her days in her home province. Most of her old friends in Nova Scotia had died, she pointed out, and Howard and I both live in small, isolated communities, a two-hour drive apart. Neither of us had neighbours or amenities within walking distance. If Mom moved in with one of us, she would be alone most of the time because our children have left home and we're at work most days.

"What would I do all day?" she asked. If she moved into one of the Nova Scotia care homes, she would have to start making friends all over again, she said.

All true. We could envision the days being long and lonely for Mom if she was isolated from her Newfoundland social circle, her beloved physician, her childhood church, and her familiar surroundings.

## Get Me on the List

Here's where to start in each Atlantic province when a family member needs long-term care:

**NEW BRUNSWICK:** Department of Social Development
www2.gnb.ca/content/gnb/en/departments/social_development.html
**General information:** 1-855-550-0552 or 211
**Toll-free:** 1-866-444-8838 for long-term care options

**NEWFOUNDLAND AND LABRADOR:** Health and Community Services
gov.nl.ca/hcs/long-term-care/
Contact your doctor or nearest hospital
**SeniorsNL:** 709-737-2333; toll-free: 1-800-563-5599;
email: info@seniorsnl.ca

**NOVA SCOTIA:** Department of Health and Wellness
novascotia.ca/dhw
1-800-225-7225 or 211 for provincially funded long-term care facilities
**Private facilities:** call individually
**Subsidized seniors' housing:** NS Department of Housing and
Municipal Affairs
Regional offices are listed in telephone book government pages and at
housing.novascotia.ca/programs/housing-programs-seniors

**PRINCE EDWARD ISLAND:** Health PEI
princeedwardisland.ca/en/information/health-pei/home-care-program
902-368-6130 or 211

See Appendix A: Continuing Care in the Atlantic Provinces, page 219, for more information.

And there was another problem: in Nova Scotia, people on the waiting list for long-term care can list several homes as their preference, but they have to accept the first available placement or they will be removed from the list. That practice didn't appeal to her, nor did some of the homes themselves. She had visited a few that had appalled her with their small, dingy double rooms, cluttered hallways, constant smells of boiled dinners and un-flushed toilets, and the listlessness of the "inmates"—as she called them.

"I couldn't live if I ended up in one of those places," she said.

I had to agree.

Other Nova Scotia facilities were more promising, but the wait was potentially several years. When Mom mused that she'd like to move to a particular residence a few blocks from her house in Newfoundland—"Just for this winter, mind you!"—I looked up the phone number in my daybook. I'd spoken with the administrator at The Home (to protect Mom's privacy I won't name the facility here) during earlier investigations, trying to discover what they could offer Mom if she decided to move from her house.

"Do you want me to call them?" I asked.

"I'll drop in to see them when I get home," she said.

I didn't believe her, expecting that she would delay and forget and change her mind again. But—to my amazement—she did drop into the office after visiting a friend who lived at The Home.

She'd like to move in, just for the winter, she told them. The staff was ecstatic that she wanted to stay with them. She was already a familiar figure there, having visited on behalf of her church and to see old friends who'd already made the move.

But when the administrator of The Home called a few months later to offer Mom a place, she turned it down. She wasn't ready, she told me later.

"Not yet."

We prepared ourselves for the eventuality that Mom would fall ill or fall down the stairs. The ambulance would cart her off to hospital, where she would spend a long time waiting for a space in a nursing home; when she finally got one, she'd live out her final days far away from family and friends. It was a pattern we'd seen among extended family members, and that we'd heard freely discussed at wakes and funerals.

CHAPTER 4

# *Might as Well Laugh*

—❖—

*F*or at least five years before Mom's 90th birthday, we continued to make light of our "Mom Stories."

"Might as well laugh. No point in crying," was our mantra. We remembered Mom saying exactly the same thing when her own father began "losing it," in the words of my brother Bill.

We'd laughed when my uncle had found Gramps sitting on his city veranda—"the bridge," as he called it—wearing a suit, tie, and hat, with his shoes polished to a mirror brilliance and his suitcase beside him. "What are you doing, Skipper?" my uncle had asked.

"Waiting for the boat to Labrador," was the reply, in a tone that said, "What does it look like I'm doing?"

We'd chuckled when Gramps had gotten angry at another uncle—one Gramps believed was captain of the ship on which he was a passenger. The skipper wouldn't let the old man pee on the deck.

And we'd laughed again when we'd heard that Gramps had answered the phone in such a mumble that the caller rushed to his home, fearing the old man had suffered a stroke. Nope. He'd dropped the phone and picked up his slipper to continue the conversation.

Mom's current situation—coating the chicken in dish detergent, hoarding plastic bags, and repairing furniture with Kleenex—had not yet reached the same level as her father's. Or had it? It was still easy enough to laugh about it at this point, but when would the situation become a crisis, demanding action?

This question whirled though my mind on my last night at my mother's house, keeping sleep at bay until it was time for us to get up and leave for her birthday party in Nova Scotia. I looked around one more time, memorizing the scene, before I locked up.

Mom was leaving for good. She wouldn't be returning to live there. I knew it in my bones, but I don't believe it crossed her mind. It was just another trip across the Gulf of St. Lawrence to see her family. A gulf—in more ways than one.

A neighbour drove us to the bus terminal on the other side of the city. The bus would deliver us to the terminal dock, where we'd board the ferry to Nova Scotia. On the Nova Scotia side, we'd catch another bus for the three-hour ride to a town near my home, where we would be picked up for the half-hour car ride to our destination.

Oddly, the neighbour who drove us to the bus had, of late, become one of the targets of Mom's unreasonable anger, and no one knew why. My brothers and I had always appreciated and remarked on the couple's generosity and kindness to Mom, and before this sudden outbreak of antipathy, she'd invariably bought gifts for them while visiting Nova Scotia. The neighbour and his wife wept over the estrangement when I visited them—a visit which aroused intense jealousy in Mom. She watched me from her chair by the kitchen window as I climbed back through the snowbank between the houses.

"What were you telling them?" she demanded when I entered.

Dumbfounded, I replied, "Just chit-chat."

"I suppose they sucked all kinds of information out of you," she sneered, muttering several insults.

I lost it. For the first time in my sixty-plus years, I chastised my mother. I told her the neighbours had always treated her kindly, and that she could not have lived in her house for so long without their help. I reminded her of the many times they'd brought her meals. Just a week before, they'd delivered a portion of their ham dinner to her.

"Enough for three meals," she'd crowed at the time.

In our daily phone chats, Mom had often described their gifts of fresh berries or tomatoes. But now she refused to admit that any of it had happened. Frustration, anger, and shame clamoured for space in my head, with little room left for patience. I told her I would hear no more derogatory comments about them.

And I didn't.

When I finished, I wished I hadn't said any of it. I was sorry—not for saying the truth, but for thinking it would make a difference. I half-expected Mom to refuse to come to Nova Scotia with me. She tossed her head, thinned her lips, and stared out the window. After a few moments of silence, I changed the subject and she reverted to good cheer. Neither of us ever mentioned my tongue-lashing. I didn't forget it, but I think Mom did, although the point of my scolding stuck. For the rest of my visit, Mom told me how lucky she'd always been to have such good neighbours. She actually went to their door to wish them farewell. That's when the man offered us a drive to the bus terminal. Aboard the bus, all the way to the ferry, Mom sang his praises.

For the first time, it occurred to me that one benefit of dealing with a forgetful person is that they can't remember the bad or the good. Still, I found it strange that Mom could be so angry at the neighbours for years without knowing why. She didn't remember their kindness, but she did remember that she wasn't supposed to badmouth them to me. Did her thoughts get stuck on a narrow spur line off the main track, needing a little shock to jolt them back into position? It was a puzzle—one I later discussed with friends who'd experienced similar issues with their aging parents.

"They go in loops," one friend commented. "Whatever you're talking about—and it could be almost any thing at all—as soon as the subject reminds them of what they have stuck in their heads that annoys them, they loop right back to it."

That sounded like Mom.

"She says such awful things about people," I complained.

"Remember, she doesn't mean it," my friend advised. "She really doesn't know what she's talking about. Don't believe her—but don't tell her that. Just change the subject."

During that trip back to Nova Scotia I didn't have the benefit of that friend's wisdom. I became exasperated with the constant repetition, which, since Mom tended to compensate for her deafness by raising her voice several decibels, was loud enough for all the passengers to hear.

At one stop, an elderly woman boarded and sat opposite us. She was well dressed, with elegant makeup, fashionable luggage, and a certain amount of confident flair. Next to her peacockishness,

Mom looked like a drab little sparrow in her faded navy coat and pilled woollen beret.

"I'm 88," the woman proudly told the ticket agent.

Mom sniffed, loudly.

"I got her beat," she said to me, in what she thought was a whisper. It wasn't. The ticket agent covered a grin. I closed my eyes.

"Well, I do!"

"Yes, Mom, you certainly do," I agreed.

"What?"

I had to repeat what I'd said, very loudly—and so our conversation went, all the way to the ferry terminal.

"The bus windows are dirty."

"It's the road salt, Mom."

"What?"

Repeat.

"They should wash them."

"They probably will before the next trip, Mom."

"What?"

Repeat.

"My legs are getting cramped."

"We're almost there, Mom," I yelled. "You can stick them out in the aisle if you like."

"Someone might trip over my legs and get mad at me."

"I'm sure they'll understand."

Not only did they understand, they could hear every word we said. If any of the other passengers was stupid enough to trip over Mom's legs after our top-of-the-lungs theatrics, they deserved to fall on their face. I'd had easier trips with my three kids when they were all toddlers!

At the ferry terminal I bought our tickets and handed Mom her boarding pass. Within minutes she had misplaced it. After a fruitless search, we returned to the ticket office to have the pass replaced. Good thing it was Newfoundland and Labrador, where the agents remembered her from her many ferry trips, and where the other passengers remained calm in the knowledge that the boat wouldn't go without them.

Once aboard the vessel, Mom found the lost pass in her coat pocket. She'd looked there before, but had pulled out only a hand-kerchief, and I wasn't about to insult her by sticking my hand in her pocket. I'd know better next time—if there was a next time—I vowed. I carried all our documents from that point on.

An old hand at crossing the Gulf aboard every ferry that ever plied those waters, Mom steered me toward a line of seats that she promised would be quiet. She was correct. Her memory worked sometimes, or the information was deeply engraved in her brain. We'd chosen a night voyage that would connect us to the only westbound bus on the Nova Scotia side, but we hadn't reserved berths.

"The seats are comfortable," Mom said. "I'd rather sit in them. It's only six hours. Why waste the money on a berth when you only have six hours to sleep?"

It made sense. It was also my own preference as I rarely slept on the ferry, whether in a bunk, or in a chair or on the floor. I'd tried them all.

On one side of me, a group of twentysomethings laid sleeping bags on the floor under the seats, crawled inside them, and began to snore as soon as the ferry left port. On the other side of me, Mom tilted her chair back and raised the footrest, wrapped her blanket around her, closed her eyes, and went out like a light. I followed suit, except for the part about going out like a light. I wiggled and squirmed under the flimsy blanket, tossed this way and that, and slept for maybe a few minutes. Eventually I got up and went to the washroom then returned to the lounge to stand at the window. I watched, in the glow of a searchlight perched somewhere over my head, as the ice parted before the ship's steady onward motion, creating ominous booms throughout the vessel. I returned to my seat and tried to read by flashlight. I wriggled and squirmed some more, then finally gave up and put the book away. I curled sideways in my seat to face Mom.

I'd rarely—or never—had the opportunity to observe her at rest. When she's awake, emotion or concentration animate her expression. She had always smiled, laughed, and frowned readily, talked a lot, and rarely slept when anyone else was awake. The family joked that she feared she'd miss something.

It was as if I'd never seen her before.

She looked...old.

With her head tipped back against the seat, gravity pulled the skin from her face to sharpen her pudgy nose and high, round cheekbones. The effect smoothed out the deep lines across her forehead and at the corners of her eyes. Her mouth was closed, but the corners of her once-full lips sagged toward her now-angular jaw. Her normally weather-beaten cheeks had a yellow, almost transparent look, like a figure in Madame Tussauds wax museum.

Dear little Mom! A wave of compassion and love swept over me. She was about to turn 90, and she was worn right out.

In that moment, I vowed she would have care. She could not, and would not, return to live alone in that big, unwieldy house.

I obsessed over Mom's future for the remainder of the night. When the sky lightened, I went to a window to look for land in the distance and was surprised to see it on both sides of the vessel. We were already sailing into Sydney Harbour. Maybe solving Mom's future would unfold in a similarly simple manner, I thought fancifully. Maybe the answer, like the shoreline, was closer than I imagined. Maybe steady forward progress, like that of the ferry, would get us there.

I won't say that was the last time I worried about Mom, but it was the last time I stayed awake all night worrying. What would be would be. If Mom's memory loss and her sudden and unaccountable—to me, at least—distaste for certain people and situations were traits of the real woman, I thought she must have been under great stress all her life to keep the brakes on those angry thoughts and feelings.

On the other hand, if the behaviour was not the real woman, something was wrong and she needed space in her life to address it. Had mini-strokes or little tumours given rise to cognitive problems? Did she have Alzheimer's or some other disease? The doctors would find out, I decided. Meanwhile, we had a 90th birthday to attend and I would pretend everything was normal until it was over. I would remember her the way she used to be. It was likely the way she still saw herself.

~*~

*I didn't know how I'd achieve my goal of finding Mom the care she needed.* The work involved in just researching the options was daunting. It would involve restarting my searches in two different provinces, crawling through the red tape of two different health-care systems, and chasing person after person who might have answers, but who would—I expected—pass me on to someone else. As a newspaper reporter, I was accustomed to digging for information—and doing it to meet urgent deadlines. But the hunt for information had never before been this personal.

First I would have to uncover Mom's financial situation. She'd never divulged any information and it was, I'd always thought, none of my business. That meant contacting Mom's lawyer, and I didn't know who they were or where their office was. Plus, it was tax time. What would I do about her taxes?

Then there was the rest of the family, scattered all across the country. I would have to ensure that Mom's only surviving sister, my brothers, and our other family members were all on side with any plan.

The most important consideration—or challenge—would be persuading Mom that any of the options, or any combination of them, would be in her best interest. I hate conflict at the best of times, and all my life I've caved before Mom's stubbornness and determination. Now I cringed at invoking her anger. It was possible that she could become so angry she'd never speak to me again. Having witnessed a friend's pain when she became estranged from a family member who'd been moved to a nursing home when all other options had failed, I didn't want to endure the same situation.

On the other hand, I reasoned, it was better for me to endure Mom's wrath than to let her break a bone in a fall, or to see her wither away alone or burn the house down around her, possibly taking a firefighter or two with her. Such occurrences were not just my imagination; I'd known them to happen—the stuff of bad-news stories.

┌─────────────────────────────────────────────┐

### Types of Care

**Seniors' housing/independent living:** Typically, an apartment in a wheel-chair-accessible building suitable for independent adults who can care for themselves but who wish to avoid home and property maintenance.

**Assisted living:** A small apartment or room with options for laundry services, housekeeping, meal services, medication management, bathing assistance, transport to medical appointments, on-site hair care, on-site entertainment, and recreation programs.

**Nursing home:** A single or shared room in a facility offering around-the-clock medical and personal care, as well as meals, laundry, and housekeeping for dependent adults. Clients may have different levels of mobility.

└─────────────────────────────────────────────┘

*A full day after leaving Mom's house, and five days before the big birthday splash we'd organized, we arrived at my place in need of a good rest before diving into party mode.*

Some party guests had arrived early, intending to beat a severe weather system working its way across the continent. Others would squeak through a few days later, on the heels of the same snowstorm, struggling through unplowed roads to make it to the party on time. Nellie, who would celebrate her own 90th birthday in a few months, flew in from Montreal ahead of the storm to stay with her granddaughter in a nearby town. She would share a chalet with Mom for the party—a chance for the two of them to relive the good old days.

As the storm travelled from west to east, it reached Newfoundland just in time to make it impossible for many of our guests to get off the island. In St. John's, my brother Dave and members of his family scrambled to change flights and book alternate routes to avoid the blizzard. Some people got through, but others got stranded in airports and motels.

Enough family members arrived early to decorate, run errands, and play endless Scrabble games with Mom. I was thankful for their presence. My own age was showing; I felt tired, a little overwhelmed by the activity, and concerned for Mom's future—a worry I hadn't yet expressed to my brothers.

On the morning of the party, my stylist friend trimmed and curled Mom's sparse hair into a work of art that Mom soon flattened with a head scarf. Family members fussed over her clothing selections like a bunch of mamas over a bride. My daughter showed Mom how to effectively wear her favourite shawl, but photos from the party showed it slung around Mom's neck like a hefty winter scarf. The photos also depict her as a proud matriarch, seated by the chalet's huge fireplace, surrounded by three generations of descendants. Maybe I'm the only one who noticed her occasional expression of, "Where am I and what am I doing here?"

By that morning, the storm had given way to bright sunshine and clear skies, but many roads, including the steep driveway to the resort, were still unplowed. Vehicles that couldn't make the slope were parked at the bottom and the occupants hiked up the hill, until Howard's SUV was pressed into service as a taxi.

Despite the travel challenges, almost all of Mom's children and grandchildren made it to the party. All six of her great-grandchildren were there. Cousins and nephews and nieces and their in-laws, students from Mom's college housemother days, colleagues from her working years in Quebec, children of old friends who'd passed away, and new friends she'd met during visits to her children all gathered at the hilltop resort near us to celebrate ninety years of

Mom. Three adult grandsons flew in from Ottawa in the morning, drove a rental car to the party, and then drove back to the airport that same evening so they could get to work the next morning.

Mom was suitably impressed! The weather had kept many people away, so we had more than enough food, rooms, and chalets available. The resort provided what seemed to be an unending parade of catered food, including a cake with Mom's picture on it. The noise level was uninhibited, to say the least, with lots of vibrant chatter, cameras flashing, and people coming and going. We'd planned for speeches and stories about Mom, but everyone was too busy catching up with everyone else. Some conversations picked up exactly where they'd left off years before, as if no time had intervened.

Then, after the youngest guests finished presenting a magic show engineered by my daughter, Mom stood up to say "a few words." I had known she would want to do just that. My gut churned with fear as I worried she'd lose her place in the middle of it, perhaps embarrass herself, and maybe get angry or sad.

Worry proved, as always, to be a waste of time.

This was the woman who, since her toddlerhood when she'd played church by preaching to her sisters' dolls, had never been at a loss for words. I sat in relieved awe as she thanked everyone for coming and made a short and moving speech about the importance of family and friends and of loving each other. I wish I or someone else had recorded it. Mom didn't use a script or notes, so we don't have any record of it.

As far as most people were concerned, Mom's speech marked the end of the party. It was already two hours past the afternoon time slot we'd booked at the resort, but the staff didn't seem to mind, as they'd seemed to enjoy the spectacle as much as the guests.

The crowd moved to the chalets, where the oldest guests watched through the huge windows as the young and young-at-heart played in the snow until dusk. The adults shovelled snow into waist-high launching pads. Youngsters—and some oldsters, including me—piled onto sleds, and with a mighty shove, zoomed down the long steep hill toward a faraway line of trees, all of us screaming in delight. At the bottom we rolled off the sleds to trudge back up the hill. The thrill and the fresh air were exhilarating and worth every step of the return climb.

We'd planned a potluck progressive dinner for the evening meal, in which guests would move among the chalets for the various courses. There was enough food for a battalion, made more delicious by the announcement that Mom would, in due course, welcome her seventh great-grandchild.

A cousin set off a massive display of fireworks, worthy of Ottawa on Canada Day, and then the excitement gradually settled down. The youngest children were put to bed and the oldest—Mom and Nellie—held court in their chalet until well into the night. Around 11:00 P.M., my husband and I drove the fifteen minutes to our house, fell into bed fully clothed, and slept like rocks.

We awakened to guests arriving at our house for coffee, breakfast, and a visit, having checked out of the chalets early to start their homeward trek. Coffee and conversation flowed freely. The whole party, including Mom, eventually moved to our house. (Nellie had snagged a ride to her granddaughter's home before catching her flight back to Montreal.)

The remaining guests spent the day playing in the snow and the sunshine. Mom picked a snowball fight with her great-grand-kids, a battle that lasted until she tumbled into a drift and had to be pulled out. She pretended that she'd done it on purpose—and maybe she had. We weren't sure, so we coddled her, wrapping her in a blanket and settling her into a lawn chair perched in the sunny lee of the house where she could watch the shenanigans and drink hot tea. It was a nice, but still wintery cold, day. Before long, Mom moved indoors to take a nap.

She stayed with us for several more days and took two naps almost every day. I didn't know if it was her usual pattern, or if she was worn out, or if she just wanted "alone time," but we let her do as she wanted without fuss. The woman was officially 90, after all.

## CHAPTER 5

# How to Eat an Elephant

~·❦·~

*M*om's changed circumstances, and the fact that I would have to take responsibility for her financial affairs by obtaining power of attorney, came at a difficult time in my life.

There never is a convenient date for sudden responsibilities, but I was overwhelmed at that particular point. Multiple work deadlines loomed. Projects that I had postponed because of my preoccupation with Mom's birthday now demanded my immediate attention. Business invitations and meetings, as well as personal appointments, filled my calendar. And it was tax time—a mathematical and logistical nightmare for a self-employed writer.

Our house was the epitome of disorder, thanks to weeks of working and doing party preparations while ignoring all but the basic necessities of laundry, cooking, and cleaning. My husband is an excellent cook, but his idea of putting things away is identical to Mom's. He places everything right where he can see it so it's available for the next time he wants it, even if that's two months hence. Thus the couch, chairs, floors, countertops, and every other surface was piled with a confusing jumble of dishes, clothing, papers—you name it—and surrounded by dog hair and muddy footprints. It would have driven me nuts, except it got the blind-eye treatment because I had no time to deal with it.

On top of my home and work challenges I struggled with nagging feelings of anger and guilt for not having recognized Mom's needs months, or even years, earlier. This was all compounded by a strong dose of desperation about her future. What could we do? Or, more accurately, as the ball was in my court, what was *I* going to do? And how?

My own self-pity infuriated me; I knew it was a total waste of time and energy that would be better spent trying to solve the problem. Nevertheless, I wanted to cry. I wanted to scream and stamp my feet. For a nickel, I would have run away from home at that point and never come back.

Predictably, no one stepped up with that nickel.

In the end, I took my own advice—advice I had gleaned from personal experience and which I often freely share with others: things could always be worse. Just breathe. Keep putting one foot in front of the other. You'll get it done.

Eventually, that's true—but it helps to know where to place the first foot.

It would be like eating an elephant, I thought. One small bite at a time.

~*~

*Thankfully, my brother Howard and his wife, Lois, took Mom to their* place in Halifax while I tackled my own most pressing tasks—and Mom's. I made lists, one for each day, and ticked off the jobs as I completed them. I attended all the work-related meetings in my calendar and advised colleagues I would be absent for at least a month to attend to personal matters. I submitted my work projects before their deadlines, cancelled or postponed engagements for the next two months, returned all urgent phone calls and correspondence, paid all my bills, and prepared a box full of my tax items to deliver to the accountant once it was certain all the paperwork was there. I got examined and fitted for new glasses. I even housecleaned—without all the planned sorting, but I put everything in its place. Most importantly, I applied myself to finding alternate living arrangements for Mom.

At the same time, Howard and Lois continuously discussed the topic with Mom, piling on the persuasion. She shouldn't have to live alone in that big old house at her age, nor should she have to clean, cook, and lug firewood, they reasoned. She deserved a rest after years of looking after others! It was time for her to have someone wait on her, right? How did she want that to happen?

It was a brilliant approach—suggesting that Mom deserved something better than her current circumstances.

We discussed tactics by telephone every couple of days, and then Dave or Bill or I would talk to Mom to reinforce the progress. We figured the decision had to come from Mom—and we were right.

After dithering (again!) over where she wanted to live, Mom decided she'd stay in Newfoundland. She had friends there, her doctor was there, her church was there. She'd move into a place just for the winter and, if she liked it, she'd stay. She explained it all apologetically, as if she thought we'd be upset at her decision to live away from us.

We figured if she had to explain it to us, she'd already persuaded herself.

When Mom made her announcement, I suddenly remembered a conversation I'd had with her when I was five or six years old. Mom and I had spent a long afternoon together baking cookies with no interference from my father or my three brothers. Dad was off on a mission, and the boys were probably napping, so it was just us girls. Mom was being teacherly and warm, devoting her complete attention to what I was doing. She let me measure the flour and other ingredients and helped me mix and roll out the dough. She demonstrated how to dip the cookie cutter in flour before impressing it on the dough, and how to move the raw cookie to a metal baking sheet—which she allowed me to grease. She showed me how to read the thermometer on the oven in the wood stove, and got me to help her add wood to make the stove hotter. There were no admonitions, no criticisms, no conflict, and the cookies turned out well. It's odd that I don't remember what kind of cookies they were, but I do remember that I wore my favourite red sweater—and that I was ecstatic with my success at baking. I wanted more days like that with Mom, and told her so in the only way I knew how.

"Mommy," I said, "when I grow up, I want you to come live with me in my house."

I remember her giving me a one-armed hug because she had something in her opposite hand. "Oh, my dear, you're some sweet. But when I get old, I'm going to live in a home just for old people."

I was hurt until Mom explained that when children grow up, they don't need their old mommies and daddies to live with them.

"I will so need you," I argued.

"Probably not, but we'll talk about it more when the time comes," Mom said. It would be another forty-five years before we even touched on the subject again, long after a lot of water, some of it quite turbulent, had run under the bridge.

Now, here we were. The time had come. Mom had come full circle, right back to her long-ago plan to move to a "home just for old people." My mind, however, had completely changed! No longer did I need her to live with me, nor did I think it was even feasible.

—◆—

*She was ready to go that very day, but first we had to find her a place.* We feared that if she settled back into her house for even an hour, she'd change her mind again and never move.

"Hang on to her until I find her a spot," I told Howard.

We knew keeping Mom in one place wouldn't be easy. She had already stayed in Nova Scotia longer than usual, and she'd soon be fed up with both Howard's place and mine. Before long, she'd be champing at the bit to get back across the Cabot Strait to Newfoundland.

But it's weird how things happen. Keeping Mom in Nova Scotia suddenly got easier when she fell ill with a severe respiratory infection. As Nellie had come down with a similar illness upon her return to Montreal, we concluded they'd both picked up a bug during the party. We didn't want them to be sick, but if Mom was going to be ill, it was better that it happened while she was staying with Howard—a physician. A strange kind of blessing!

Howard and Lois nursed Mom back to health in their home, refusing to let her leave for a couple of weeks until a doctor (not Howard) deemed her well enough to travel. Unbeknownst to Mom, of course, no one was doing any deeming until I could find a new living arrangement for her in Newfoundland.

It had been at least a year since my last contact with the provincial housing agencies of Newfoundland and Labrador, and my notes had vanished into the mess in my office.

Mom had rejected an earlier offer from The Home, which, in Nova Scotia, would have placed her at the bottom of the waiting list. I didn't know what the Newfoundland and Labrador policy was, so I decided to start again from scratch. I searched through online resources to gather a list of phone numbers and names, including some that were familiar. I called all of them, leaving messages on answering machines all over the island. I described Mom's situation to everyone and anyone who answered, working on the principle that if you throw enough mud at a wall, some of it has to stick.

Once all the mud was in the air, so to speak, there was nothing to do but wait. Meanwhile, Lois kept working on Mom, telling her how convenient it would be to have someone else do her laundry, make her bed, and cook her meals. It was time Mom had a break, she argued.

She played the card of Mom's illness as an argument in favour of finding new digs.

"Imagine if you were all alone and got sick like that," Lois suggested. "You didn't even know how sick you were. We were the ones who noticed your breathing was funny. Who would notice you were sick if you were all alone?"

Oh, Lois was good. She repeated the comments every time it seemed that Mom had forgotten, until the idea imprinted itself in Mom's mind and she began to speak of it as if it had been entirely her own idea.

During this time, Nellie's illness had prompted her to move from her Montreal walk-up apartment into a seniors' complex. She called Mom to tell her how wonderful it was.

Pat, Lois's mother and also Mom's good friend, had made a similar transition the previous fall. After initially bucking the move to a nursing home, Pat had settled in as if she owned the place. She extolled the virtues of her new home, persuading Mom of its advantages. It was a nice place, Mom agreed after a visit—but a bit too fancy for her.

She was going to move into The Home in Newfoundland, she announced, out loud, to everyone in the family.

She spoke as if she'd made the decision herself that very minute, with no prompting and no previous discussion. It appeared that she'd forgotten she'd already told us her preference, and that we'd agreed to look into it for her. It was also possible that we were moving too slowly for her and she felt we needed a reminder. Who could tell?

She had friends and relatives there, she reminded us. And she knew everyone there, residents and staff, because she'd volunteered there for years. Barely had the announcement passed Mom's lips when the rest of the family accepted it as a done deal. She was going to move.

Hallelujah!

Memory loss teamed with stubbornness doesn't always lead to a positive outcome, but those two traits clinched the decision for Mom. She couldn't remember that Lois had worked hard to persuade her: the decision was hers alone. That was the memory. And now that she'd made the decision, there was no going back. That was the stubbornness. When she talked to me about it over the phone from Howard's place, she spoke as if she needed to persuade me. I let her explain all the reasons for the move.

It was the wave of the future for Mom's cohorts, and she would join the throng. She couldn't stay in the house any more, she told me. Could I help her move?

Could I help her move! *Oh, please God, let The Home have an opening!*

Those were my thoughts as I said "O-kaaaay" in a semi-reluctant tone that led Mom to try to persuade me more vehemently.

I promised to talk to the people at The Home, to clear the decks to take her back to Newfoundland, to stay to help her get settled. I didn't tell her I'd already been working on it for weeks.

Gradually, the people I'd been calling began to call me back. I was able to tell them that Mom had decided she wanted to move into The Home, not into one of those places that had a name like a spa in the Alps. Finally, on a Friday morning, I got a call advising me to phone Western Health's Assessment and Placement Services that very day and ask for an intake worker named Georgia. She didn't answer, of course, but I left a message. Telephone tag was becoming my new favourite sport.

Georgia called me that night as I was climbing into bed—close to midnight Newfoundland time. She'd been working at home on Mom's file, she told me. If I could call The Home first thing Monday morning and ask for Diane, she was pretty sure they'd have a place for Mom.

Never did a weekend grind past so slowly! It was worse than waiting for Christmas. Fearful that I'd sleep through "first thing Monday morning," I awoke at 4:00 A.M. I washed the previous day's dishes, swept the floors, made coffee, read the news, made breakfast and ate it, and put the dirty clothes in the laundry. I stared at the clock, and then at the phone, and then back at the clock.

Eight o'clock was too early, I told myself, pacing between windows to stare outside for inspiration. The staff at The Home would be busy giving everyone breakfast. I needed to be sure that whoever I talked to actually had the time to talk, so, when 8:30 came, I told myself to wait another twenty minutes.

There is no explanation for what happened next.

Instead of listening to my own reasoning, I suddenly reached for the phone, dialled The Home, and identified myself to the woman who answered.

"Is Diane there?"

"Thank God you called!" she exclaimed. "This is Diane. I've been trying to reach your mother for a week. I have a room here for her. If I hadn't got hold of her in the next twenty minutes, it was going to have to go to the next person on the list."

I immediately understood that Mom had secured a room at The Home—but the words that echoed most loudly in my head were "twenty minutes."

If I'd waited the twenty more minutes I'd promised myself, Mom might have been waiting for twenty more weeks! I fist-pumped silently as Diana described the room they'd prepared for Mom. It was a single room in a quiet wing, with big windows and a view of the garden and forested hills behind them.

"When can she move in?" she asked. I was doing quick calculations in my mind.

"A week from Wednesday? If the ferries are on time?"

~ ✦ ~

*It would take me that long to tie up loose ends, fetch Mom, make the* reservations, pack, and arrange transport to and from the ferry on both sides of the Strait. The bus was not an option this time—too tiring for someone who had just been ill.

My brothers and I had once calculated that, in the years since Mom had first emigrated to Canada from the (then-) British colony of Newfoundland, she'd probably tripped across the Cabot Strait close to six hundred times. She'd made another twenty or so trips by steamer across the Strait of Belle Isle and up and down the Labrador coast. She'd travelled with our father and with us, and later, after Dad died, by herself as she visited her children, grand-children, and great-grandchildren on the mainland. Probably only commercial truckers and the ship's crew had made more Cabot Strait crossings than she had.

Mom knew all the best places to take a snooze on every New-foundland ferry that ever sailed over those decades. She knew which toilet doors would slam on your ankle if the ship tossed as you entered, the spots on the deck where a person might trip, the best place in the dining room to get noticed by the wait staff, and how to beat the rush to the car deck when the ferry docked.

Her shipboard experience made her free with both criticism and advice for Marine Atlantic, the Crown corporation that operated the service for much of that time. Restaurant prices gouged passengers, the ankle-crushing doors were dangerous, the gift shop should sell locally made items, lounge ventilation was poor, there weren't enough puke bags for seasick youngsters, empty lounges should not be locked when others were overcrowded, liquor should not be served to people who were about to drive vehicles off the ship and down a moose-plagued highway, the Swedish-made seats were designed for Vikings instead of ordinary-sized people (and they didn't recline far enough), and the lounge television sets were too loud for people who wanted to sleep. Sometimes Marine Atlantic even acknowledged her suggestions and made improvements. It's been a long time since a toilet door has swung shut on my ankle!

The crew must have cringed a little whenever they saw Mom's name on the passenger list—but she outlasted most of them. She'd seen generations of officers and crew come and go.

Even with her poor memory, she could identify our particular ship by its lounge furnishings alone, and could point toward the bow or the stern to direct me toward toilets hidden along obscure corridors.

She liked to get on the boat just before the 11:00 P.M. sailing and wake up on the other side at 5:30 A.M., just in time to visit the washroom and disembark—where a bus would be waiting outside the ferry terminal to carry passengers to points across the island. But this time I wanted Mom to have a daytime ferry crossing, because she needed her sleep. Another reason? I sadly realized it might be her last trip.

It had been many years since she'd made a daytime voyage. By daylight, I told her as we boarded the ferry, she could watch the Nova Scotia shore slip away, look out for St. Paul Island and passing ships, and examine the horizon for the first view of the rugged Newfoundland mountains. She was unimpressed! For her, the trip was simply a means to an end, but for me, it was a joy. I preferred day crossings, and thought of this as a mini-cruise: a time out to think and not do much else, with no work or social demands. I liked to eat in the ship's dining room and watch the horizon dance up and down past the windows. I liked chatting with the crew and the other passengers—and imagining their stories. Like Mom, I had never been seasick in my life and saw no reason to start.

But although they were interesting, day crossings came with a problem. There was no bus or train connection that matched ferry departures or arrivals on either the Nova Scotia or the New-foundland side. My husband had driven Mom and me to the North Sydney terminal early in the morning; he'd stayed overnight in Cape Breton to visit his brother, then made the three-hour trek home the next morning in a terrific rain-and-snow storm.

On the Newfoundland side, arriving passengers had to either stay the night in Channel–Port aux Basques to catch the bus in the morning, or arrange for a private ride to their destinations. Mom's younger sister, my Auntie H., had lived in Port aux Basques for her entire married life, and her son and daughter still lived in the area. I called both cousins ahead of time to see if they had room for us. The family was accustomed to such requests, and had developed a routine around checking weather, tides, and vessel arrival times.

Both households kept food stashed for travellers' lunches, and they even had favourite parking spots at the terminal where they could be easily found by disembarking passengers. I don't know if they were resigned to their fate as occasional hosts or if they enjoyed it, but their hospitality made trips across the Gulf much more enjoyable.

My cousins both said yes to my request for lodging, and even argued over who got to keep us. In the end, my cousin John met us. He and his wife had recently built a state-of-the art home outside town and they wanted us to see it. It was as beautiful as he'd promised. In the interest of family peace, he also made sure we had a brief visit with his sister, Fran, and her husband—on a street that twisted around rocks and coves to a glorious spot within spitting distance of the ocean.

In the morning there was a surprise: the loan of Auntie H.'s small car for me to use until I returned to Nova Scotia. She was still "down south" in Florida, where she'd gone for the winter, and wouldn't return to Newfoundland for several weeks. So away we went, driving just ahead of the storm that had plagued my husband's drive home from Cape Breton, and which was now making its way to the southwest corner of Newfoundland.

## CHAPTER 6

# A Room of Her Own

❧

"Let's eat out for dinner," Mom said, as Corner Brook came into view. "I'll shout you to a meal."

In other words: her treat. I envisioned McDonald's, but no. She directed me to a proper sit-down family restaurant in a hotel with a hilltop view of the city. It was busy, but we got a table by the window. I ordered cod tongues, a delicacy from my childhood that happened to be a menu special that day. They tasted so good I almost cried.

During the meal, people came to our table to say hello, exclaiming how long it had been since they'd seen Mom: proof that she hadn't been out much in recent years. Some diners had been students when Mom had worked at the college; others knew her from church or other organizations, or from her neighbourhood. They had to tell her who they were, and I could see some were taken aback when Mom didn't recognize them or remember their names.

"I don't know who that was," Mom whispered loudly, of a woman who'd introduced herself just minutes before. "I had to pretend I knew her."

No one but Mom was fooled by the pretence but, by that point, I was of the "so what?" mindset. If people talked, they talked. They could come back when they were 90 and tell me how much they remembered.

Our bellies full, we left the restaurant for the fifteen-minute drive to The Home. Halfway there, Mom cleared her throat.

"I want to stay in my house tonight. I don't have to move into The Home right away."

My heart almost stopped. Of course, everything to that point had been going far too smoothly! I negotiated a turn in the road before I answered.

"Oh, Mom, the house is too cold. The heat's not on, and there's no food there."

"But you're going to stay there," she said, logically.

I'd been wondering if I should, but I hadn't made up my mind. Cousin Marg, who lived two blocks from The Home, had offered me her spare room. "I'm staying with Marg," I said, deciding on the spot.

"I'll stay with her, too," Mom said. I could have argued that Mom hadn't been invited, but I knew that Marg—generous Marg—would take in half of Newfoundland if they landed on her doorstep.

*Dear God, help me out here,* I prayed. But suddenly, I didn't care. I was tired of caring.

"Okay," I said. "When do you think you might like to move into The Home?"

"Oh, tomorrow. Next day. Maybe the day after." Mom was using the smartass tone of voice she normally reserved for police officers when they nabbed her for speeding, or for landowners who'd caught her walking past their "No Trespassing" signs. Spoiling for a fight.

I didn't take the bait. "Good enough," I said. "Just keep in mind that I only have a few days to help you get settled. The longer you put it off, the less time I have to help you after you move in." I could imagine her delaying things for weeks.

"When do they expect me?"

"Today." I'd already told her this several times over the past week.

"They do?"

"Yes."

Mom squirmed a bit in her seat.

"Maybe we could just drop in on the way to the house," she said, finally.

"Sure."

I had just enough time to signal and make the left turn into The Home's parking lot. Mom got out of the car and trudged to the door as if it was just another day and she was making her usual visit. I followed.

The lobby was full. The residents had just finished dinner and were milling about, some perched in the few available chairs, and others seated on their walkers.

"Anna!" they exclaimed, almost in unison, when Mom walked in the door. "We missed you!"

"Where have you been?"

"Are you really coming here to live?"

The exuberant welcome gave Mom pause, just as a pleasant-faced woman in pink scrubs bustled from the door marked "Office."

"You're here!" she grinned. "Oh, Anna, wait 'til you see your room. It's beautiful! Come see."

Mom allowed herself to be led away. I followed, down a wide, bright hallway and around a corner.

"Here," the woman said, stopping at a door and twisting a key. She flung the door open. Mom stood with her eyes wide and her mouth agape, looking for all the world like one of the shepherd children seeing Our Lady of Fátima.

While neither holy nor virginal, the room was truly a pleasant vision: pale yellow walls, white trim, light blue carpet, a twin bed, a nightstand, and a tall wardrobe. Floor-to-ceiling sliding doors revealed a huge closet, and another door opened to a tidy bathroom with a toilet, sink, and shelves. A wide window collected the early afternoon sunshine, providing an aura of comfort, light, and peace.

"It's all mine?" Mom asked from the doorway. "Just for me?"

"Yes, my dear. It's been painted and they laid a new carpet—just for you."

Mom walked in and sat on the bed, plopping her purse beside her. The motion brought to mind a story my parents had often told about me as a five-year-old. At the end of an arduous cross-Canada journey that had involved multiple trains and boats and lengthy delays, I'd walked into our newest house, plunked my little green travel bag onto the kitchen table, and announced, "I'm here now, and I'm staying here for a good long time!"

I vividly recalled the feeling I'd had all those years ago—and I was relieved to see that Mom appeared to be feeling the same way now.

"I like the bedspread," she said, bouncing a bit. "Is it mine?"

"Yes, my love, unless you want a different one," the woman replied.

To me, the bedspread was a dreary mix of dull blues and greys—the only drab spot in the room—but I didn't argue. Mom liked it.

"Now, Anna, you just missed dinner. Would you like something?"

Mom assured the woman that she'd eaten, and named the fancy restaurant for good measure.

"We'll have afternoon tea in a couple of hours, so you'll be able to see everyone then."

"I'm going to visit them right now," Mom announced, rhyming off the names of her friends at The Home, and then added, "Monica! I'm going to stay here, okay? You can bring my things in from the car. We'll get the stuff from the house later."

Why had I ever worried? Silly me.

Leaving Mom to poke around in her new digs, I went to the administration office where I wrote a year's worth of cheques from Mom's account to pay for her keep, printing "PoA" after my signature each time to indicate that I held power of attorney. (When Mom had first made out her will more than two decades earlier, she'd made me executor and assigned me power of attorney. This would turn out to be an essential step when it came to my managing her affairs.)

> ### *Power of Attorney*
>
> Power of attorney is a document that gives another party legal authority
> to act on a person's (the donor's) behalf, in order to manage his or her
> legal and financial affairs. The power given can allow complete control
> over all the donor's finances and property, or it can be limited to a spe-
> cific task. It is considered crucial when planning for future incapacity
> or long absences from home. A person must be mentally competent to
> grant power of attorney. All types of power of attorney become invalid
> when the donor dies.
>
> (Source: lawdepot.ca.)

I added some money to a "comfort fund" to cover any extras
Mom might need, signed some papers, received some information,
and made some notes before collecting Mom's bags from the car.

When I got to her room, she wasn't there. She was out visiting
her friends, a staff person in blue scrubs told me. "Do you want
me to find her for you?"

"No, thank you. I'll just leave her a note with the bags and
come back later."

It was a good sign that Mom was too busy to worry about her
bags, I thought, as I drove the kilometre to her house.

~❦~

*My mother's house is one of just six houses on a short street that ends in
a cul-de-sac, halfway up a hillside so steep it's impossible to build
a house opposite her place—so she has an astonishing and unin-
terrupted view of the bay.*

Across the still, deep water, the hills rise, rank upon rank, from
a deep green forest with its pale necklace of villages and patches of

snow-covered meadow, to lighter greens, and then into the misty grey-green-blue of the distant mountains. On the near shore, homes and businesses follow streets that twist around rocky outcrops and ford innocent-looking brooks that can, and sometimes do, become torrential floods.

Below the house, on the opposite side of the cul-de-sac, the hill drops steeply to the old narrow-gauge railway bed. As children visiting our grandfather, my brothers and I counted railcars from the upstairs windows at night, and from the bridge during the day. If it was a long train, we could see the engines trundling eastward, over the crossing on the other side of the valley, before the caboose wound around the back of the hill to reach the track in front of the house.

The "Newfie Bullet" had long been retired when I returned with Mom that spring, but the steep slope both above and below the old railway bed remained. Only a few trees have ever been able to grab a footing there. The hill offers a view to the far end of the bay where the sun rises, its rays striking Mom's house before they land on any other home in the city—or so I have believed since childhood.

Invisible from Mom's house, tucked under the brow of the hill, are more houses and a tangle of streets and lanes reaching down to the cove where the brook, which long ago carved out the valley below, meets the bay.

A lifetime ago we dallied in the cove while walking back to Gramps's house from church on summer Sundays. Sometimes, if it was hot, we were allowed to strip to our undies and jump into the water. Gramps once kept a dory moored there, which he used to row "out the bay" or "up the bay." On one of our annual summer visits, our whole family landed in the cove in a friend's seaplane, creating a bit of a stir as we waded ashore through the shallows. Near the cove there was a well-used ball field; now it's just a place to drive all-terrain vehicles. A yacht club and a picnic park take up most of the shore where we once played and swam.

It is a hard climb up the hill from the street to the back door of the house, exercise which kept Gramps trim, I figured, and maybe wore out my grandmother's heart before her time. A few years before Mom turned 90 she'd hired a man and his bulldozer to make a driveway all the way up the hill to the back door. She didn't use it in winter for fear she'd get her car stuck.

When I arrived, the calendar said "Spring," but it was still winter in Newfoundland. I had to park at the bottom of the hill and slog through the waist-deep snow, a remnant of Mom's birthday storm. Luckily, she'd left a shovel outside the house, and after thirty minutes of digging I had cleared a narrow path from the car to the door.

A month and two days after Mom and I had left the house for Nova Scotia, its rooms were as cold and as quiet as a grave. I switched on the heaters and snooped around to look for some of the items Mom had requested. She wanted her "other" footwear, extra clothing, her radio, and some odds and ends. I couldn't find most of the things she wanted. For instance, there was no sign of her winter boots in the back porch, in the front hallway with the other outdoor footwear, or in any of the bedrooms. (They would turn up much later—in June—along with a lot of other missing items, wrapped in a plastic bag in the woodshed, damp and mouldy, zippers rusted beyond use. I found her ski jacket in June as well, in a bag that had fallen behind the freezer in the porch.)

Mom would have to make do with what she had—the too-big green polka-dotted neoprene rain boots she'd worn to Nova Scotia, a pair of black leather sneakers with duct tape across the soles, and a red plush jacket she'd taken from my own "giveaway" pile at home. The jacket looked cozy, but it was unlined, cold, and impractical. Mom wore it over her full-length quilted winter coat and also over her pyjamas, as the spirit moved. She told all and sundry that she didn't know where she'd gotten it but it was the best coat she'd ever had.

She looked a bit like Elmo from Sesame Street, but I was long past caring what Mom looked like. When I was a kid, she'd worn black-and-orange gum rubber boots to church, their tops turned down like those of a fisherman just off the trap boat. Everyone, and I mean everyone, knew she was my mother and teased me about her. She rarely combed her hair, preferring instead to cover it with outlandish hats. Not for her were the more refined Jackie Kennedy–style scarves favoured by my friends' mothers. Mom owned—and often wore—a Sherlock Holmes–style deerstalker, a lime green straw pith helmet wrapped in a monstrous cream-coloured ribbon, a hat made in the North of white Arctic fox fur and decorated with the black-tipped tail of a winter weasel, a multicoloured tam-o'-shanter that had been part of her curling regalia in Saskatchewan when I was a toddler, another tam in quilted Newfoundland tartan, a knitted Viking-style helmet with braids that hung almost to her waist, a black-and-white houndstooth fedora, and toques and berets of every colour. She mostly wore berets, using two hands to snug them into the correct position: above her rather large ears and tilted rakishly over her forehead.

She'd told us all our lives that if she didn't wear a hat she'd get sick because her hair was too thin to keep her head warm. As a child, I'd privately believed that she'd rubbed off all her hair by constantly wearing a hat, indoors and out. I changed my theory when I met one of her bald aunts. It's a good thing my brothers and I inherited Dad's thick mop.

I collected a few berets for her, as well as some pyjamas— without holes and with all their buttons—a housecoat, some tops, slacks, sweaters, underwear, and several intact pairs of socks, and delivered them to her that afternoon at The Home.

Supper (in Mom's parlance) was still two hours away, so we spent that time making lists of what she'd need: among them, her reclining chair, her television, her radio, and her toiletries. It would take several trips to collect it all, as Auntie H.'s car could only hold so much.

Finally, Mom went to supper, and I went to Marg's. She and her husband wined me and dined me, and gave me a warm and peaceful bedroom where I slept like the dead. I woke up the next morning feeling refreshed.

~❦~

*The next week was a whirlwind of activity. I felt duty-bound to document* every action I took on Mom's behalf—a job in itself. I spent the days getting Mom organized and settled, and the nights and early mornings tapping away on my laptop at Marg's dining room table or in bed, as I had an important work deadline.

The Home's administrators suggested it would be practical to buy a small bar fridge so Mom could keep cold drinks, fruit, or treats brought in by visitors. They advised that she should also have a small table with a couple of straight chairs in case she wanted to sit and write, play cards, or have tea with a visitor.

"Take the chairs from behind the dining room table," Mom instructed. "They're in good shape."

Using Marg's SUV, we delivered Mom's wide-screen television, her recliner, and the only two un-broken chairs we could find: original Bass River arrow-backed specimens with dirty cushions. The cushions went into the first of many garbage bags I would end up filling before returning to Nova Scotia.

Two similar chairs, also pushed into the gate-leg dining table that had been my grandmother's, had wobbly legs and loose backs. A decorative chair we discovered at a jury-rigged desk at the end of the upstairs hallway had seemed like it might work in Mom's room, but when we moved it, we discovered that the seat was broken completely in half; it had been strapped together with a man's leather belt and the repair disguised by a flouncy cushion. There were also two folding chairs that seemed to be made exclusively for pinching fingers—unsuitable!

There were two decent tables in the house, but both were too big for Mom's room. One was the long kitchen table that Mom had rescued decades earlier from someone's garbage. She'd replaced the broken top with another person's discarded hardwood flooring, which she'd then polished to mirror brilliance before covering it with a pink floral vinyl tablecloth. The other was my grandmother's gate-leg table, which Mom wanted Marg to have—although Marg had no space for it.

We took Marg's SUV and headed uptown, shopping list in hand. Eventually, among all the clunky furniture, which took up a lot of showroom space for so-called minimalist styles, we found an elegant, well-made walnut table with fold-down leaves. It suited the arrow-backed chairs and would fit perfectly into the allotted space.

As we delivered it, I realized something: "Mom, it's the first new table you've had in your life!"

"Is it?"

We counted through the years. Throughout her governess and college years, and as a missionary on the Prairies, Mom had lived in furnished rooms and owned no furniture at all. She and my father had lived in furnished houses all their married life, and any time they'd needed a table someone had loaned them one or Mom had salvaged an old one. After Dad died, Mom had lived in furnished rentals until she'd retired to the house her father had built.

She triumphantly remembered she'd had one new table: Gramps had made it as a wedding gift for her and Dad.

"But that was a coffee table," I protested, remembering it well: handmade of Newfoundland birch with a grey marble-look Arborite top. My brother Bill and I used to push it across the hardwood floors in our Saskatchewan house, with our two youngest siblings, Howard and Dave, perched on top. We pretended it was a car and we were taking them for a drive.

It went with Mom whenever we moved and it followed her to The Home, too. It proved perfect for raising her new bar fridge to a height that was easier to reach. The space under the table was designated for storing shoes and slippers, and for the newspapers Mom couldn't bear to part with.

"I might need them to start the stove," she reasoned.

"You don't have a stove here."

"Oh, I don't, do I? Well, someone else might need them. Ask Marg, would you?"

Staffers at The Home promised to keep the stack under control.

"We have our ways," they said. I suspect they pulled a few from the bottom whenever they cleaned.

During my week and a half in Newfoundland I visited Mom at least twice a day, but I avoided spending long periods at The Home, hoping this would give her more opportunity to meet other residents and socialize. I didn't want her to miss my presence when I left.

Also, I had a lot to do in those ten short days.

## CHAPTER 7

# *House of Surprises*

~❦~

W hen I was not running a multitude of errands or trying to meet my
work deadlines, I tore apart my mother's house to find any
important items that Mom may have forgotten about, or might
soon forget about—including money.

I had no method; my goal was just to find out what Mom had,
so I would know what she needed, and to deliver to her any items
she might need right away. One of her visitors from the previous
summer had seen Mom hiding bills in a dresser, so I wanted to
find any money before an intruder did. I discovered that Mom
had stashed enough cash throughout the house to pay for the bar
fridge, the table, a new telephone, and a lamp—with some money
left over for her wallet.

I searched for documents, family keepsakes, seasonal clothing,
and Mom's missing footwear. I crawled under and pulled out beds
to search behind them. I emptied every drawer, cupboard, shelf,
closet, plastic tote, suitcase, bag, and trunk, and spread their contents over tabletops, beds, chairs, and on the floors—on the princi-

ple that if everything is out in the open it is easier to sort and deal with. (A year later, I discovered that Japanese tidying guru Marie Kondo, author of *The Life-Changing Magic of Tidying Up*, approved of my method!)

I found things no one knew Mom even owned. Under a bed, pushed back against the wall, I found a brand new blue gingham comforter, still wrapped in its original plastic, packed tightly into a suitcase. Thinking it would match the carpet in her new room, I took it to Mom.

"You went out and bought me a quilt!" she enthused.

"No, Mom, I found it in the blue bedroom," I said.

"How did it get there?"

No answer.

On my next visit I delivered a white faux-fur parka, which had been carefully wrapped and squeezed into another suitcase under another bed. Mom had given me an identical one for Christmas several years earlier, and had given a blue version to my brother Bill's wife, Jeanette. Mom had obviously purchased this third one, but had never worn it or given it to any intended recipient.

"It's beautiful. Do you want it?" she asked me.

"No, Mom. I have one like it at home," I said. "It's yours. Put it on."

It was too big for her. The "Elmo" jacket looked better, but that didn't stop Mom from twirling through the halls to show it off, with me following closely behind to catch her in case she actually levitated mid-twirl and crashed.

"Look what my daughter got for me!"

I smothered my laughter.

When I visited her a year later, she gave me the coat. "Someone gave this to me," she said. "I'll never wear it. You take it." I tried it on, twirled around in it, and thanked her effusively. That evening, when a neighbour visited Marg to collect items for a church bazaar, I gave her the coat—with a warning. "Don't let Mom near that sale!"

We all giggled.

Right now, though, it was no giggling matter. Mom's house was full of things that she couldn't possibly live long enough to use, and neither could her three generations of descendants. What could we do with it all?

The easy answer was to send it all to the dump, but to me that route didn't honour Mom's efforts to preserve the items in her possession and care. Everything had to be sorted and examined, because if Mom had kept it, she'd kept it for a reason, even if it was a nutty reason. If she'd intended to give something as a gift, I could fulfill her wishes. If the reason was that she simply couldn't bear to throw it out, then I could do that for her, too—after determining whether it had historic or family significance, or some intrinsic value that was not immediately obvious.

I understand Mom's mindset because I share it, too. To me, broken or found items might be turned into funky lamps or unusual towel rails. A piece of driftwood might be an artist's version of a soul twisted in hell—or maybe it's a sailboat. A gold-plated platter is, after all, gold! People go to a lot of trouble to get gold. On the other hand, sometimes a broken light bulb is just a broken light bulb—but a decision still has to be made.

My mother's house held a lot of decisions—and surprises—for me. The biggest surprise was Mom's bed.

Since moving in permanently when she'd retired, Mom had always used the big bedroom at the top of the stairs, sleeping in a three-quarter–width bed with an antique metal frame of the sort that often lives out its usefulness as a fence or a gate in a rural garden. The metal was shaped into a heart just above her pillow, and the bed had decorative brass knobs on each corner post. That was all fine—but then came the mattress and bedspring.

Mom had complained every morning for a few years that her back was sore. Every time she did, I told her to buy a new mattress. "It *is* new," she always replied. What she had failed to reveal was this: Mom's "new" mattress was a 39-inch (twin sized) mattress that had been laid atop a sheet of plywood that had been cut to the same size as the mattress. This all rested on an old-fashioned 48-inch (three-quarter–sized) coil spring base that went with the antique metal frame. Therefore, both the mattress and the plywood sank several centimetres whenever Mom got into bed at night.

Because the plywood was nine inches short of covering the spring, Mom had moved the mattress-plywood combination to the outermost edge of the bed, leaving a gap between the mattress and the wall, which the bed was pushed up against. To fill that gap, Mom had arranged empty shoeboxes like LEGO blocks—side by side and end to end, atop the spring. Then she'd flung a ripped bedspread over the whole construction, taking care to hide the jagged tears against the wall.

Without pulling back the bed covers, one would never have known that the mattress was too small for the bed, or that my mother had rolled over onto shoeboxes every night for God knows how many years.

I couldn't believe it. My mother slept on shoeboxes! She could afford to buy a larger mattress—she just refused to spend the money. It defied logic, and it perturbed me more than anything else I'd encountered in my mother's house.

A close second perturbation, though, was the sorry state of the walls and the floors, which became increasingly evident as I moved items around. Carpet extended just a couple of centimetres over a closet floor that had no wood at all under the layers of flooring, a situation once hidden by a box. Behind a wardrobe, wallpaper peeled from damp plaster; a shower curtain covered rust on the side of the tub; water-stained ceiling tiles were not-quite-disguised by a hasty paint job. Dust curled, a centimetre thick, along the tops of picture frames, above doors and windows, and on any baseboards that were hidden behind beds and chairs.

To be fair, if I had walked out of my house as suddenly as Mom had walked out of hers, a critic would find plenty of dust in my wake—but not quite so much and not in quite so many places.

"Mom must believe man is made from dust," I commented to Marg as we spent an evening removing books from the shelves that filled a wall in the living room. "She'd have a whole posse with all this."

We sneezed together.

We inspected each book in case Mom had hidden money or papers in the pages. We found, instead, just damp and mouldy paper. That mould could be deadly stuff, so, after carefully shaking each book, we put it directly into a garbage bag. (These were just generic old books—not a rare or valuable tome among them.)

~⚘~

*As the days wore on, the sorting continued. Alone at the house, I looked* through thousands of photos, making it a rule that I would keep only the ones that were in focus, with recognizable people in them, with information written on the backs, or that dated back to the early days of Newfoundland photography.

A cache of Girl Guide photos, badges, and documents from the 1930s included an image of Mom with the organization's founder, Lady Baden-Powell—quite a find, in my view. Recalling that Mom had told stories about meeting Lady B-P, as she was called in Guiding circles, I set the treasures aside for my niece, Sally, a Guide leader and history buff.

I extended the leaves on my grandmother's big dining table to make room for three piles—one for each brother.

A couple of weeks after my departure, my brother Dave would be the next person on scene, his daughter Sally with him. They would take the pile I made for them, plus whatever they and their families wanted, and clean out the storehouse and the woodshed. Both outbuildings had been buried under two metres of snow while I was there.

"If no one wants the skis that are in the storehouse, I'd like to have them," I told Dave.

"All I want is some old hardwood flooring Mom has in there," he said. He admitted he'd been coveting it for years, but had been hesitant to ask. Obviously, at this point, Mom couldn't use it.

After Dave would come Howard and Lois, who promised to sort through the linen closet. I'd started to pull out all the tablecloths, napkins, blankets, handmade quilts, sheets, and pillowcases, but put them back because I'd had no time to sort through them.

"Make sure you take anything you want," I told them.

I doubted whether Bill would come to look through things, as he lived farther away. But you never knew with Bill, so I started a pile for him anyway. Ultimately, I shipped it to him via Canada Post, in two monstrous parcels.

But meanwhile, it was just me. One day, while sorting through Mom's jewellery—which hung from pegs and sat tangled inside little boxes and bags in her dresser drawers and in the white leatherette box that Dad had given her when I was about ten—I found her missing sterling silver cross. It designated her as an associate member of the Toronto-based Anglican convent of St. John the Divine.

Mom had never been a bona fide nun—just an associate, because, she'd always said, she couldn't even contemplate a vow of celibacy. The comment always raised shocked giggles but it was, I believe, the truth.

Mom had lost this cross several years earlier and had eventually purchased a replacement. Now she had two. Aside from her gold wedding band and her ordinary little watch, the only jewellery she regularly wore was her St. John the Divine cross. It belonged to the order, and was to be worn until her death, when it would have to be returned. Would we have to return both of them? It was a bridge we would have to cross at another time.

I removed most of the costume jewellery, leaving the best pieces in the box with the cross, and delivered the box to her room. "You found the cross!" Mom exclaimed; her memory suddenly acute. She fingered the jewellery. "I have some nice things, don't I? Would you like something?"

I suggested she portion the pieces to her grandchildren, but said I would like to have one of the plain little wooden crosses.

"My dear, it's yours. Here, take it." She thrust it at me. "Maybe I should go to the house to see if there is anything else special to give away. And I'm missing some clothes," she said.

Of course she was.

I feared she'd want to move back into the house if she visited, but there was no legitimate reason to keep her away. It was hers.

"It's a mess," I warned as we parked at the bottom of the hill.

"It was tidy when I left it," she said.

"I know. I made the mess."

Inside, Mom reacted oddly to seeing her possessions pulled out of their hiding places and into the middle of each room. She reached out and made tentative plucking motions with her hands without actually touching any of the purses, knapsacks, brand new blankets and towels, souvenirs, photos, high-tech toys, gift bags, walking sticks, and other unearthed items. She seemed surprised, as if she'd never seen these things before. Indeed, many items were still in their packaging, with labels attached—having arrived as gifts or as impulse purchases that had been stashed and forgotten.

Except for the clothes I had already delivered to her at The Home, I'd sorted and returned her "good" clothing to her dresser and to the closet in her room. She rooted though these to find her favourites, but I called a halt when she started collecting the stained and torn clothing from the discard pile on the floor.

"Why do you want that stuff?"

"They're my working clothes," she said, looking at me in puzzle-ment. "I might need them for painting or working in the garden."

I just looked back at her, wondering what to say, or whether to comment at all.

"Oh," she finally added. "I guess I don't need them."

"No, you are now a lady of leisure, and you deserve to be. You have a lot of nice clothes! Wear them; don't waste them."

Put to her like that, the high queen of anti-waste couldn't refuse.

"Anything that anybody gave me over the years, give it back to them if they want it," Mom instructed. She left it to me to figure out who had given her what, a process that would be aided by my copious lists.

"You know, I think we might as well sell the house," she said, not for the first time, as we continued to sort through her things.

"That's a good idea, Mom."

After Mom returned to The Home that day, Marg and I sorted through the clothing Mom had left behind. We removed everything from all the dressers and shelves.

"Stained or ripped or no buttons or the zipper doesn't work? It goes in the garbage," Marg instructed firmly as she held up a sweatshirt I'd put in the bag to give away. She turned it toward me to show a large stain on the sleeve. "Not to the Salvation Army. Would YOU buy it?" It was a lesson learned—one that I carried home with me and that I intend to follow for the rest of my life.

Eventually we delivered ten large bags of clothing to the Salvation Army Thrift Store downtown. Marg and I also sent twenty-five garbage bags of expired food, broken household items, mouldy books, and soiled and torn clothing and bedding to the dump.

---

## Where to Take Used Items

- Thrift stores like Salvation Army, Value Village, local second-hand stores
- Antique shops
- Specialty shops for used records and CDs, books, sports equipment
- Church rummage sales or bazaars
- Red Cross or fire departments that support families who have lost their homes
- Post on Kijiji, Facebook Marketplace, or other buy-and-sell sites
- Do it yourself: hold a yard sale or garage sale

---

*My next visit to The Home began like this: "Monica?!" Mom's requests for* me to do something for her always started with my name, followed, to my ears, by both a question mark and an exclamation mark.

"You look after your father's war stuff!" she ordered. "Take it with you!"

"Where is it?"

"It's in a metal box in my bedroom," she said. "You look after it."

She couldn't tell me what she meant by "look after it."

"Whatever you're supposed to do with that kind of thing," she answered, waving her hand dismissively.

I found two locked steel boxes, neither with a key. I broke into them and, sure enough, one held Dad's medals and ribbons, a deadly-looking knife, his release papers and, of all things, a marlinspike for doing something to horses' hooves. Dad had showed it to my brothers and me when we were young, while he polished his medals for Remembrance Day. The marlinspike had been issued to him when he'd entered the Royal Air Force in the early days of the Second World War, before Canada had its own air force. We thought it odd that fly boys would be expected to care for horses, but assumed it was a British thing.

The other box held love letters to and from Mom, newspaper clippings, and other personal papers. I stuffed it all into my suitcase to sort out later.

~❦~

*After Mom's clothing, her important documents, and most of her personal* items had been sorted and distributed, my immediate job at her house was complete.

I found a wheeled hockey equipment bag that could hold all the documents I wanted to take home with me; it could also hold a few other bits and pieces that would cushion their ride. Into another wheeled suitcase went two quilts and some items my family had given Mom over the years. Among them were a finger-painting by my granddaughter, a carving of Jesus in a fishing boat that my son had given her, and a set of books that Lois and I had scoured bookstores and the internet to find as a birthday gift. She had said she wanted them, but their covers weren't even cracked. I planned to read them before passing them along to Lois.

By that point I had two large wheeled suitcases chock full, plus my carry-on bag and a sling bag that doubled as a purse/laptop bag. Labelled with bright red HEAVY tags, the big suitcases would cost extra to lug home by bus and ferry, but it was worth the expense, as they would give me a head start on the paperwork that would await me the next time I went to Newfoundland.

I could drag nothing more back to Nova Scotia on this trip. I left behind—for my next trip—a dresser I'd always declared would be mine someday, recognizable by the black splotches on the mirror and a stain from nail polish that Marg's sister Clare and I had spilled some forty-five years earlier. I'd piled more documents and some household items on top and in the drawers and taped a big note on top: "For Monica."

Marg and I defrosted the refrigerator and the freezer and moved all the remaining useful items to Marg's. We turned down the heat, leaving it just warm enough to keep the pipes from freezing. My very last task was to turn off and empty the leaking hot water heater. I called an expert—Marg's husband—who ran a drain hose out the back door and down the steep hill into a snowbank. The next people at the house would have no hot water, but neither would they have a massive puddle across the floor.

Finally, it was time to leave. I said goodbye to Mom, Marg, and everyone else, parked my aunt's car in Marg's driveway, and took the bus to Port aux Basques. I would leave Newfoundland on the overnight ferry.

It would be another night without sleep.

## CHAPTER 8

# The Banker and the Cable Guy

~·~

*M*oving Mom involved more than simply installing her in new digs and distributing the contents of the house. Her swift transition from independent living in a two-storey house to a single room with me looking after her affairs had left a number of bureaucratic loose ends.

These included the bank account Mom had opened at the same bank I used in Nova Scotia about thirty years earlier.

"For emergencies," she'd said. She meant her emergencies, not mine, but she'd made me joint owner of the account.

A certain sum had been automatically deposited each month; the money had been left mostly untouched, because even when she visited she usually carried enough cash to cover every possibility. But once in a while she'd get me to withdraw funds in order to do her bidding.

"Monica?! Would you get some of my money out of the bank and buy something for [insert name]'s [birthday/Christmas/Easter/anniversary/graduation/whatever] gift?"

I'd ask her how much she wanted to spend, what she had in mind, and then I'd shop. The task got much easier after the introduction of online banking. I'd use my credit card to buy the item online and have it delivered directly to the recipient if possible. Then I'd transfer money to my account to pay for it. The account never held more than a few thousand dollars, which, I assumed at the time, represented a large portion of Mom's retirement stash.

In addition to that account, Mom also held investments at that particular bank, about which I knew next to nothing. It had been her business, not mine—until a letter had arrived for me, shortly before Mom's 90th birthday. An investment had matured and I (or Mom) needed to act. Apparently, I was a joint owner. This had been news to me, although I must have, at some point long ago, signed for it. The bank's financial advisor suggested in a phone call that, given Mom's age, it would be best to deposit the investment into Mom's account.

On one hand, I was amazed that Mom had had the forethought to invest money—and to add someone else's name to the account. On the other hand, I was concerned because at that point she'd forgotten she had it. But of course, so had I!

I'd made an appointment for us to meet the advisor at the bank during Mom's 90th-birthday visit. The young woman verified Mom's information on the computer by asking her a variety of questions: birthdate, full name, address.

"Is that right, Monica?" Mom asked after each response.

Finally, the advisor, who appeared about the age of my oldest grandchild, asked for a piece of identification with a photo. Mom and I looked at each other.

Mom's last passport had expired decades earlier, and she'd had no need to produce such identification since her long-ago trip to England and France. She fished through her wallet, pulling out a stack of plastic. They represented fifteen years of work identification cards—the most recent photo taken when she was 65.

"They're expired," the advisor said. "Do you have a current driver's licence?"

Why hadn't I thought of that? "Oh, yes, of course," Mom said, fishing some more. She pulled out three cards and tossed them on the desk. She was getting a bit snippy.

The advisor sorted through them.

"They're all expired," she said. Indeed, Mom's most recent driver's licence had expired almost two years earlier.

"It must be good. I was driving with it up 'til last month," Mom said. The advisor and I exchanged glances. She primly closed the file folder.

"I'm afraid I can't do anything more without current photo ID," she said. I showed her the document I had that said I had power of attorney.

"I'm sorry. She still needs a photo ID. The computer won't accept anything else." She suggested we get some photo ID and return.

We certainly wouldn't be coming back to that bank, Mom informed the advisor. She was speaking for herself, not me, as I'd done business there for forty years. In fact, I'd dealt with that bank since I was 9 years old, although at a different branch, when Dad had marched me into the grand pillar-fronted edifice in the town where we lived and set me up with a savings account. From that point on, I'd received an allowance from my parents: a portion had to go into the bank, a portion had to go into the offering plate at the church, and the rest was mine. I still keep the habit, in varying degrees.

No doubt Dad wanted no daughter of his to grow up as ignorant about handling money as Mom had been. She'd never written a cheque until after Dad died; she used to take her chequebook to Dad and get him to fill it in and she would sign it. Her method for handling money was to spend only cash and to make sure she didn't spend all of it. But if the amount she'd managed to stash in her investment account was any indication, that system had worked for her for a long time.

And my system worked for me. I wasn't about to switch banks because Mom had no photo identification.

I told Mom we'd make the necessary adjustments at a branch in Newfoundland. "You'll come with me back to Newfoundland?" she asked.

"Yes," I promised—for the fifth or sixth time.

"I am never using this bank again," Mom announced loudly as we walked past the lineup on the way to the exit. The financial advisor wore a pained look as, I'm sure, did I.

The disappointment that we'd been unable to adjust Mom's bank accounts was secondary to the revelation that Mom had been driving without a licence for two years. Holy cow! I was still in shock as I walked out of the bank. My head felt disconnected from my body. Imagine if she'd had a crash! Maybe she had, given the battered condition of her car. I tried not to think of my mother as a hit-and-run suspect.

A few days later, I privately approached a higher-up official at the bank who knew Mom personally to ask if they could address her banking situation before she left Nova Scotia. Thankfully, they could. Nothing was said to the youthful financial advisor—who had, after all, only been doing her job.

Once we were back in Newfoundland and Mom had moved into The Home, we set out to rectify the ID card situation. Marg and I took her to the Newfoundland vehicle registration office to remove the registration from her car, which was unfit to drive, and to have a government photo identification issued. When she eventually received the permanent card in the mail, she kept the temporary one she'd been given, "Just in case I lose one," she said. I wanted to suggest that she keep them in separate places, but refrained.

When Mom had moved into The Home, I'd thought it would be wise for her to keep the same telephone number she'd had at her house for the past twenty-five years. That way, I wouldn't have to advise the whole world of her new number, and Mom wouldn't have to try to remember it.

I'd called the phone company. After spending hours on the phone, getting transferred from person to person, and explaining the situation over and over to people who seemed to have no idea what to do, I decided that it might be easier to get action by calling the phone company's courtesy desk than by dealing with its billing or accounts departments. I was right: a pleasant woman answered and easily made all the arrangements; she also offered suggestions for dealing with Mom's account in future. She had gone through a similar task with her own mother, she said, and she knew exactly what I needed. I emailed her a digital scan of the power of attorney document that I had already stored on my laptop, and the process moved like a hot knife through butter.

The actual telephone number would be changed to Mom's new address, the billing address would be changed to mine, and the installation would take place the very next day. Marg and I dashed out to buy her a new telephone, as none of the phones in the house worked properly. Each of Mom's two portable phone bases had three handsets; most of the numbers were worn off the keys. When Mom had been living there, the handsets were rarely set on the matching charger, and generally only one base was plugged in at a time, and then often to a power bar that was switched off. If the phones had lost their charges, only the corded phone in the bathroom would work—but the moisture in the room created staticky transmission. Mom had two other corded phones, but neither worked; their casings were cracked as if they'd fallen from a great height or had been thrown against a wall. Either was possible: Mom's favourite expression for something that didn't work was: "I'd like to put a boot to it."

At least twice during the previous year Mom had summoned telephone service technicians to repair a phone that was simply disconnected. "A lovely young man fixed it," she'd tell me during our next conversation.

"What was broken?"

"Oh, I don't know. He fiddled with something under the desk and then it worked. He wouldn't let me pay him. A lovely young man." I suspected a charge for the lovely young man's visit was added to her bill, but there was no gain in suggesting it out loud.

Closing the house's internet and cable TV accounts proved more difficult, much of that because of Mom's—and my—ignorance

## The Costs of Moving Mom

Packing up an entire house and moving someone to new living quarters isn't cheap! Here are just a few of the costs you can expect to encounter:

- Packing supplies: boxes, bins, tape
- Moving company or truck rental, gas, and other transportation
- Cleaning supplies
- Disconnection of city water
- Disconnection or re-routing of telephone and cable services
- Ongoing heating and electricity costs; eventual disconnection charges
- Ongoing property taxes and insurance
- Legal and real estate fees
- Emergency repairs
- Mail-forwarding fees
- Change-of-address notices
- Purchase of small furniture and appliances for new space
- Incidentals

of both systems. Her setup was incomprehensible: on the electrical side, Mom had plugged together a series of short extension cords that snaked around the walls and under the couch to connect every piece of electronic equipment, including the telephone charging base and the floor lamp, to a single power bar. It sat under the television cart in a nest of wires and cables.

The switch on the lamp had been broken for a long time, a problem Mom had solved by plugging the lamp into the power bar and using the toggle on the power bar to turn the lamp on and off. Unfortunately, switching off the lamp then also turned off the electricity to everything else in the living room: her portable phone, the modem and router, her laptop computer, her printer and her television. And because the laptop and phone continued to work as long as their batteries held their charges, in Mom's mind their sudden failures were unrelated to the power bar.

As a result, she could continue to play Scrabble from the disk she'd inserted (and promptly forgotten) when she'd bought the laptop three years earlier, but she couldn't access the internet because the modem wasn't powered. That was why she could tell me in one breath that her internet was broken and announce in the same breath that she was playing Scrabble "online." When it got dark and she turned on her lamp, everything might work for a while, but since Mom generally turned off the lights and went to bed notoriously early, there was little time for anything to get fully charged.

As a rule, it had been nearly impossible for me to figure out Mom's computer problems over the telephone, and it was not much easier in person. The confusion was confounded by Mom's lifelong habit of calling everything technical "the thing." A screen icon was "that little thing on the screen," but that could also mean the cursor, the toolbar, or the start menu. The keyboard was "the thing on the thing on the desk, you know, in front of the computer"—which meant "in front of the monitor." The only recognizable term she used was "that X thing in the corner." It was no surprise that she didn't know and couldn't describe what was wrong with her email or her Facebook page.

Usually Dave could figure it out, so he would correct the problems whenever he visited Mom. Eventually he created a remote connection so he could fiddle with her computer from his home on the other side of the island. But when Mom had begun using the power bar as the lamp switch, those repairs became more complicated. Dave tried to walk her through the process of rebooting, but his explanations were beyond her comprehension and her obtuseness was beyond his patience.

It was only now, after I untangled the wires, connected them to the correct ports, turned on the power bar, and typed in the passwords that Dave provided that I learned that she had been offline for nearly a year. No Facebook, no email, and definitely no online Scrabble!

Despite having long ago given up watching television regularly or using the internet at all, Mom had continued to pay for both connections—another situation we had not suspected, and to which she wouldn't admit.

When I discovered that The Home had Wi-Fi, I delivered Mom's computer to her, all ready to go. A year later I took it away when I found it sitting on the floor of her closet, untouched and uncharged.

"You might as well take that thing," Mom said. "I can't get it to work."

As well as Wi-Fi, The Home had complimentary cable in all the rooms, so Mom didn't need her house service moved, but simply cancelled.

The main challenge in cancelling both the cable and internet was to find out which company or companies provided those services, as Mom couldn't tell me. I dug through some bank statements to find a record of the company's automatic withdrawals (turns out it was just one company), and contacted them. They wanted their equipment returned before they would cancel. "What exactly do you own?" I asked.

It ought to have the company name on it, but it might not, said the rep as he described the parts over the phone. In the end, I dumped—into one large box—all the wires, connection boxes, modems, and any other unidentified bits and pieces I found stuffed

under the computer or the television sets in the living room and
bedroom. The box wouldn't fit in the back of Auntie H.'s car, so
Marg took it to the store in her SUV and we took Mom along for
the ride. I heaved the box onto the counter, where a floppy-haired
young man sorted through it and gave most of it back to me. The
leftover techno-junk eventually went to the Salvation Army.

At The Home, the cable wouldn't initially connect because the
previous occupant's private cable service hadn't been disconnected
from the room. When the installer and The Home's administrator
tried to address the issue, Mom got snippy.

"Poor planning, I'd say," she said with a smirk that, I'd learned
over my lifetime, could lead to a vicious diatribe about whatever
displeased her. Before any further comments could pass her lips,
the exasperated installer retreated to his truck to investigate the
situation by phone. It was straightened out within a day, but Mom
continued to blame her inability to change the channel on his installation. Finally, a staff person set the television to the regional
CBC station, and that's where it stayed.

Mom's cellphone would have to be cancelled, too, but I held
off until I was sure it was no longer needed. Dave had helped her
buy one a year earlier when Mom had dug in her heels against our
proposals to install a medical alert alarm or to hire a part-time
caregiver. She was willing, instead, she swore, to carry the mobile
with her at all times in a small cross-body purse. She promised to
use it if she fell or had any other emergency, but the only time she
actually used it was when the portable house phone was "broken"—
that is, when the base was unplugged. In the end, she rarely carried
the mobile phone. "I forget. It's here somewhere," she'd say when
I asked where it was during one of our daily phone calls. By the

## Medical Alert Alarms

Medical alert alarms are electronic pushbutton devices that are worn by the user as a pendant or a wristband which, when activated, alert family members and emergency responders. Some devices are equipped with automatic fall detectors and some work both at home and offsite. Numerous companies offer the service in Atlantic Canada, including:

- LivingWell Companion (Telus) 1-888-505-8008; telus.com/en/ns/health/personal
- Life Assure 1-800-354-5706; lifeassure.com
- LiveLife Alarms 1-888-794-4904; livelifealarms.ca
- Philips Lifeline 1-866-984-3411; lifeline.ca
- Northwood InTouch (Nova Scotia only) 1-800-461-3346; northwood.care/intouch

(For information only; please note that this list is not an endorsement of any of these services.)

time I found it hanging in its tiny purse from a nail in an obscure nook of her bedroom, the battery was dead. I recharged it and left it in a visible place in my mother's house for family use. When the house was finally empty, I cancelled it, too.

And finally, there was the matter of her bank accounts. Taking full advantage of the use of Auntie H.'s car, I toted Mom with me to her bank (a different one than in Nova Scotia). While she regaled the staff with anecdotes, they worked on gathering all her information and adding my name to her accounts. Despite my efforts to involve Mom in the transactions, she just waved her hand at the advisors and said, "Talk to Monica. Monica is looking after it all. Put her name on everything."

Then she went back to her storytelling. It was her way of signalling that things were well and truly in my hands now.

## CHAPTER 9

# Doctors and Lawyers

—❖—

*T*wo days after Mom moved into *The Home*, I went with her to a previously arranged doctor's appointment. At Lois's suggestion, I had a tax document for the doctor to sign that would certify that Mom's care was a necessary expense due to disability. Until Lois mentioned it, I hadn't been aware that this Disability Tax Credit existed. After the doctor checked for remnants of Mom's recent respiratory infection and ordered a follow-up X-ray, she quizzed Mom about her circumstances.

I had taken an unobtrusive seat in the corner of her office, as my intention was to be an extra set of ears, but not part of the consultation. The seat happened to be out of Mom's line of sight, which was a good thing when the doctor began quizzing Mom. When Mom replied that her memory was excellent, and that she never left the stove turned on or forgot where she put things, I felt my jaw drop and my eyes widen in horror. I hoped the doctor didn't believe it! A quick glance from the doctor told me that she understood, and I relaxed.

---

### The Disability Tax Credit

The disability tax credit (DTC) is a non-refundable tax credit that helps reduce the amount of income tax you may have to pay if you have a disability. The goal is to provide some relief for the costs involved in managing a disability. In order for you to qualify a medical practitioner has to fill out form T2201, which certifies that you have a severe and prolonged impairment.

(Source: canada.ca/en/revenue-agency.html.)

---

She signed the document and I later delivered it to a friend who was in the process of calculating Mom's taxes. This friend had completed Mom's tax returns for the past number of years, and she understood her tax situation much better than I ever could—and she would take no pay.

"It's my gift to your mom," she always said.

A few hours after that medical appointment I decided to scour Mom's house for her tax documents. At least two years previously I'd advised Mom to get a box, mark TAXES on it in big letters, and shove everything into it when it arrived. I found no such box. She had stashed her documents all over the place. Any document I found that wasn't needed for her taxes I put into a tote for my records, and the rest I delivered to our tax person. I would find more as I continued sorting through Mom's possessions. I may still have missed items, scattered as they were. The next year, as I organized Mom's financial documents myself in order to turn the information over to my accountant (along with my own confusing tax information), I understood what a truly great gift Mom's friend had offered.

The day after her doctor's appointment, I took Mom to the insurance company to cancel the policy on the car the mechanic had refused to safety-inspect, and which was, by that point, in a scrapyard. I also cancelled the automatic bank withdrawal for the fee, as it was entirely possible the company would keep withdrawing the money with none of us noticing. In fact, it would take quite a while for me to figure out all of Mom's financial dealings—what came into her bank accounts and what went out.

The next stop was the post office, to arrange for all of Mom's mail to come to me for a full year. My daughter, who'd moved often enough to know the ropes, suggested that twelve months would get us through the next batch of Christmas correspondence as well as the next tax season. It would give me time to discover what bills, notices, magazines, and personal correspondence Mom received so I could send out notices of her address change. The move would also alert me to Mom's contacts: her pensions and any other income or financial information, membership in organizations, other insurance policies, charities she favoured, and anyone or anything else she was in contact with.

---

### The Personal Information Kit

Regardless of age, all adults should prepare and maintain a file of information that will be useful when they move and for family and friends in the event of their illness or death. The information should list financial and personal responsibilities; identify the location of important documents, like a will; identify doctors and provide medical data; and provide other necessary information. It should be kept in the home in case of emergency, and a trusted person should know its location. A copy may be given to trusted family or friends for safekeeping.

See Appendix B: Creating a Personal Information Kit, page 223.

Mom had temporarily cancelled her newspaper before going to Nova Scotia, so I reinstated it, ordering it to be delivered to The Home. The monthly payment was charged to my Visa card, as Mom no longer had one. It had expired, and I decided she didn't need a replacement.

Everywhere I went I showed officials my copy of the power of attorney document that had been assigned to me two decades earlier. They copied it for their records, even though Mom was always there to vouch for me, should it be necessary.

But there was a small wrinkle: about ten years before Mom had gone into The Home, she'd called me to say she'd made out a new will, making both me and Howard executors and assigning me power of attorney with Howard as the backup. She hadn't told me where the new will was, so I'd assumed it would be in the same hiding place as the first one, along with the power of attorney.

When I'd gone to Newfoundland to collect Mom before her birthday, I'd found the big brown envelope exactly where, years before, she'd told me it would be. No will was included, just a certified copy of a document giving me power of attorney over Mom's affairs. Howard's name wasn't on it, but I figured that was an oversight: Mom hadn't understood, or had simply forgotten, the exact arrangements. This was the document I'd since waved around at the bank, at the telephone, cable, and internet companies, at the post office, at the insurance people, and at anyone else who questioned my authority over Mom's affairs.

Months after Mom's move, back in Nova Scotia, when I tried to change Mom's mailing address with the Canada Revenue Agency, they requested a certified copy of the original power of attorney. I had only one certified copy of the original, and the agency wouldn't accept a copy of a copy. I had to find the original.

The law firm's name was on the document in my possession. I found a phone number online, but was told that although my mother may once have been a client of that firm, she wasn't any longer. They couldn't or wouldn't tell me who Mom's current lawyer was. I called Mom.

"I don't know. Someone downtown," she said.

All the law firms were downtown, as near as I could tell. I combed through the stacks of papers I'd lugged home with me, and after two days I found an old receipt from a law office. I called that number and was told a lawyer would call me back.

Meanwhile, I could pay Mom's property taxes because I was a joint account holder on her bank account. Then I called the pension office of her former employer to try to have her mailing address changed—which they promised to do as soon as I could send a certified copy of the power of attorney document!

Around this time, Howard and Lois made their way to New-foundland to take their turn at sorting through the house and spending time with Mom—not necessarily in that order.

"Talk to this lawyer," I instructed Howard. "Play the 'doctor' card. I need to straighten this out or nothing else gets done." Howard called the downtown lawyer's office and referred to himself as "Doctor" when he left a message. No doubt he sounded much more professional than I had on my first contact with the firm, as I hadn't even known at that point whether this really was Mom's attorney, and my frustration with the situation was likely audible.

Maybe his title helped, or maybe it was just because Howard was a man, but the lawyer, Ms. M., returned Howard's call. He must have given permission for me to be involved, because then she called me. She asked me to send an image of my driver's licence to prove my identity, which I did. Finally I had someone I could talk to! It was a good thing there had been no emergency. (It was also a reminder to myself to update my own will—and to tell people where I put it!)

To my great surprise, Ms. M. informed me that the power of attorney document I'd been using was not valid; it had been replaced by a later one that named both Howard and me. She said she would provide me with copies of the new one. How many would we need?

"Three should do it," I said, explaining that the Canada Revenue Agency and Mom's pension plan were the only holdouts about changing addresses, but I assumed another situation might arise as I went along.

When she asked about Mom's house, I told her the plan was to clean it out and sell it.

Slow down, she told me, except in more lawyerly terms. It was imperative that I protect the interests of Mom's heirs and successors, she said. "Do you know the contents of your mother's will?"

Mom had told me when she'd re-written her will several years earlier, I replied. Instead of leaving everything to be divided among her four children, she'd left the house to one extended family member, with the rest of her estate to be divided four ways. More recently she'd talked about changing it back to the initial four-way division, but I didn't think she'd done it, nor was it clear to me whether she'd now be considered rational enough to make any legally binding changes. If Ms. M. would like to meet with Mom to sort out the situation for herself, that was fine with me. The lawyer said she would.

I hadn't seen the will, I told her.

"No, it's here with me," said Ms. M., adding that, for reasons of confidentiality, I wasn't supposed to see it. She went on to say that in order to sell the house, I had to have permission from the designated heir.

I would arrange for the person to contact her, I told her. I knew Mom had wanted to leave the house to this particular relative who she thought would move into it and keep it in the family. At the time, the proposed heir had agreed to the conditional bequest, largely to soothe Mom's worries. But life gets in the way of the best laid plans, and so it was with the proposed heir, whose prospects had taken a turn away from moving to Newfoundland.

The heir was immediately notified of the situation, and they officially declined the bequest in a letter that winged its way to the lawyer, copied to me, giving permission for the house to be sold.

I asked Mom later if the lawyer had called or visited her.

·"No!" she said in surprise. "Why would she?"

"Oh, when I was talking to her about documents, she wondered how you were, and mentioned that she might drop in for a visit," I said evasively.

I didn't know whether to believe Mom. Ms. M. might have visited—and Mom just didn't remember.

For his part, Howard was happy enough to let me handle Mom's affairs. He'd helped Lois sell her mother's house when she'd been in a similar situation; by the end of that process his garage was full of his mother-in-law's furniture, he was completely burned out, and he needed a break. He offered to help whenever I needed him, though, and I promised I'd keep him in the loop.

Daffodils were blooming in my garden at home by the time the valid power of attorney documents arrived from the lawyer. I quickly relayed them to the CRA and to Mom's pension plan. Dragons, slain—or the immediate ones, at least.

While my brothers visited Mom and took time to sort out the house without me peering over their shoulders, I could finally turn my attention to my own life. It was spring planting time, writing deadlines loomed, and I'd neglected my husband, children, and grandchildren long enough. I quietly promised myself I'd return to Newfoundland after the snow melted, with a truck big enough to cart away every last item that remained in my mother's house.

## CHAPTER 10

# The Sword and the Revolver

—⋅⋅—

*Y*ou can try to prepare for everything, but inevitably someone is going to throw you a curve ball. As soon as I had returned to Nova Scotia after getting Mom settled into The Home, she'd called me in a panic.

"Monica?!" Mom bellowed.

*Uh-oh, an emergency,* I thought, opening my mouth for a "What's wrong?" answer. I barely drew a breath.

"Did you find the sword?"

"Sword?! What sword?"

"Dad's sword," she replied, in an impatient tone that suggested I should have known all about it.

She meant her father, not mine, although occasionally she called my father "Dad" when speaking to me—almost as often as she mixed me up with her younger sister. This time, I knew she was talking about Gramps because I was certain my own father had never possessed a sword.

"Gramps had a sword?"

"A big sharp sword, in one of those sheath things," she added.

"A scabbard?"

"I guess. Did you find it?"

"I never saw a sword or a scabbard. Are you sure?"

As soon as the words left my lips, I regretted them. Asking someone with dementia whether they are sure of their most recent statement is like waving a red flag at a bull, or so I'd been told by more experienced friends.

"Oh, yes," was the emphatic answer. "Dad had a sword, but I can't remember where it is. It needs to be found before someone gets hurt."

"What was he doing with a sword?"

"He was King Billy."

"What?"

"In the Orangemen's Day parades. The Glorious Twelfth. He rode a white horse and he had a sword to wave around. They all had swords."

The Glorious Twelfth refers to Protestant King William's triumph over England's Roman Catholic King James II in July 1690, at the Battle of the Boyne in Ireland. July 12—Orangemen's Day—is a holiday in Newfoundland and Labrador. To me, it's a divisive reason to hold a parade, especially given that I, a Newfoundland-born Protestant, had married a Roman Catholic Cape Bretoner with Irish–Newfoundland roots.

In my grandfather's day, most non–Roman Catholic Newfoundland men were members of the Orange Lodge, so it was no surprise that he'd belonged. However, I hadn't known that Gramps was so prominent a member as to have played the part of King William of Orange in the annual parade.

I asked Mom where she thought the sword might be.

"I haven't seen it in years—never since I retired. But it used to be there when Dad was alive. I wonder if he hid it under a floorboard."

That meant the sword could be anywhere. Every second floorboard in the house creaked ominously. I had gory visions of a young family buying the house and a kid cutting off an arm or a leg when they discovered it under a closet floor.

"We'll look for it," I promised.

"He had a revolver, too."

I nearly dropped the phone. "What?!"

"Well, yes. Everyone had guns. He used it to butcher the animals. And to kill dogs."

It was family lore that Gramps had hated dogs; he called them "crackies" (the term for a pet dog as opposed to a working sled dog), and considered them to be vermin that destroyed his poultry and chased his cows. If one ran loose on his property, he figured it was fair game. The dead dogs apparently shared a mass grave, although searches by my brothers and I and our cousins had never found it.

"What did the gun look like?" I asked.

"Like a revolver. You know. A cowboy gun."

Sigh.

"Okay, Mom, we'll look for that, too."

Mom's call came in time for me to advise Dave, who was soon going to arrive at Mom's house in his pickup truck with his daughter Sally. They were going to bring their sleeping bags and other gear so they could camp in the house and sort through things day and night—a chilly proposition as there was no hot water and it was still early spring.

"I'd heard stories about that," he said when I called. "I figured they were from long, long ago. Not recent."

"Mom thinks the sword and the revolver might be in the house. Or in the woodshed or the storehouse. Or maybe they aren't there at all."

"I'll look. They might be in the same place as the marijuana."

Decades earlier, Mom's tenants had neglected to properly re-place a ceiling tile before they moved out of the house. Noticing the protruding edges, Mom had climbed on a stepladder to fix the tile and found a big bag of marijuana in the cavity. She promptly emptied the bag into the toilet and flushed, and told no one but my brothers and me.

We laughed. "She wouldn't try to flush a sword, would she?"

The house was full of hidey-holes: Gramps was said to have hidden good Jamaican rum in one such place during Prohibition. "Look for Gramps's rum, too," I said, before signing off.

Over the course of three days, Dave and Sally sorted through the remaining photos and papers I'd piled in the living room. They added to the individual family piles and took what they wanted, including the historic Girl Guide paraphernalia. Sally later scanned all the photos she and her father had removed and shared them online.

They collected all the remaining cables and wires left from those I'd gathered earlier into one large tote for further sorting; they loaded the rototiller, some tools, and the old hardwood floor-ing that Dave had coveted into the pickup.

Since Marg had no room for the big dining table, she suggested that Sally take it. Sally, however, already had a large dining table. They decided to leave it behind, but Dave took the broken chairs, as well as two old-but-useful steamer trunks, to repair in his workshop.

They also removed forty-five bags of garbage from the woodshed and storehouse, including compostable scraps that Mom had gathered over the past several winters and then forgotten to add to the garden. The muck had rotted in the bags and bore a wicked stink.

They put it all out to the curb, even though there was a limit of four bags per household, and luckily Dave was there to meet the garbage truck when it stopped in front of the house. After a brief conversation about the monumental pile of trash, the driver offered to make a second trip later that day. If he had room, he promised, he'd collect every last bag. He was as good as his word.

Dave and Sally left four separate piles in the storehouse to be re-examined: potential yard sale items, hazardous materials for proper disposal, recyclable items, and stuff for other people to claim. They similarly sorted the woodshed, leaving behind the firewood, the lawnmower and its can of gas, assorted steel and iron bits, a box of old square nails, some railway spikes, four tires, some tarpaulins, nets, rope, and other odds and ends.

Our Port aux Basques cousin John came by, looking for something of Gramps's to have as a keepsake. "Something no one else wants," he said. Appropriately, given the percentage of his boyhood he'd spent with Gramps in the carpentry shop, he went away with some ancient tools.

Not forgetting the task I'd assigned him, Dave crawled under the house via an opening under the front veranda, declaring the crawlspace empty and dry: no guns, no swords, no marijuana, no booze!

I contacted the eldest of Gramps's grandchildren, Wayne, who had grown up next door but had since moved to the other side of the island.

"Tell me about Gramps's gun and the sword," I said, after the usual pleasantries. "Mom's panicked over someone getting hurt."

Wayne chuckled; he knew Mom almost as well as we did. "Dad took the gun from him one day when Gramps was waving it around," Wayne said. "He was scared he'd hurt someone, just like your mom. The gun's long gone. I don't know where."

Wayne couldn't recall a sword at all, but I trusted his memory more than I trusted Mom's.

"Good luck," he said as he hung up.

We'd need it, I figured.

~᛫~

*I'd left a scribbler on the kitchen table at Mom's house so family members* could leave each other notes as they processed the house's contents. In addition to his amusing comments about booze and weapons, Dave left a lengthy message in the scribbler, right after a suggestion to have all the vinyl LPs assessed for their value. Dave's note warned in large letters: "BE CAREFUL OF THE TOILET! IT WIGGLES!"

Howard and Lois arrived a couple of weeks later and discovered on their very first day just how serious the toilet situation was. The first time they flushed it, water poured down through the living room's tiled ceiling below. They suspected it had been leaking slowly for some time, as the wax seal under the toilet had completely deteriorated. Weeks earlier, Marg and I had noticed an old water stain on the living room ceiling and assumed it had come from a long-ago bathtub overflow upstairs. Turns out we were wrong, and now we no longer had a leak but a gusher. Howard wrapped the toilet in garbage bags and duct tape and put a big sign on it: DO NOT USE!

He and Lois disinfected the bathroom floor and most of the living room and opened the windows wide. "No need to go upstairs. Just relieve yourself in the corner of the living room," Howard quipped. In actuality, when nature called, he and Lois hopped into their car and scooted down the road to Marg's.

We all marvelled that no one had been electrocuted in the bathroom, given the dangerous combination of water and electricity: the toilet sat in a corner of a converted upstairs bedroom, directly above the fuse box that was situated in the corner of the living room below. The sewer drain ran down the wall beside the electrical panel.

Howard and Lois expressed surprise at the "copious amounts of stuff" still remaining in the house and outbuildings, and couldn't see how either Dave or I could possibly have removed anything at all. "You should have seen it before," I told them, but there was no doubt the pile was smaller when Howard arrived, as Dave and I could point to the records we'd kept.

Howard and Lois bagged the contents of the linen closet, boxed up the knick-knacks, took down Mom's jury-rigged shelving, and put the shelves in the storehouse along with the "cluttery" little tables and the "trippy" little rugs, as Howard called them. They took the rest of the pictures off the walls, revealing more cracks and stains, and sorted them into boxes along with the rest of the books.

"We have removed things that we wanted," Howard wrote in the notebook. He'd also removed the fuses for the bathroom because the heater switch in that room didn't work anyway, and he'd turned off the water inlet under the stairs. We didn't need another flood.

"Bones out," he signed off.

After some discussion among the siblings and the cousins, we decided against repairing the toilet or anything else before selling the house, on the principle that a buyer would probably gut the place to completely renovate, or might even tear down the house and build something new. There was no point in spending tens of thousands of dollars to make repairs and doll up the paint for little or no return. We were more in favour of reducing the price to reflect the state of the house. But the more we uncovered, the sorrier it looked.

"I don't trust the floor in that back bedroom," Marg told me. "It's scary how far it sags when you walk on it."

The chimney from the living room oil heater had once passed through that room to the roof. When the stove and chimney had been removed in favour of electric baseboard heaters, the hole in the floor had been covered with plywood and at least two layers of cheap carpet. Obviously, nothing but a full repair would fix a sagging floor—and if the floor dipped under Marg's slight weight, no one else should be allowed to even venture near it.

The kitchen floor in front of the wood stove also dipped when anyone walked on that spot. We feared that a sudden sinking of those floorboards might tip the squat wood stove far enough to spill coals and start a major blaze. Were our imaginations working overtime, or were we taking reasonable precautions? Whichever it was, we all agreed that it was better to be safe than sorry. We swore off having any more fires in the wood stove.

Gramps would have been proud of our "safety first" approach, we agreed. He was forever adjusting furniture, picking up sharp items, and building railings so no child would be injured on his watch. Mom once told me his precautions stemmed from the time her little sister—Auntie H.—had careened down the hill on a sled and plowed right into a red-hot fire iron that had been placed in the snow to cool. She obviously survived, but that scare travelled down the generations: all of Gramps's descendants are obsessed with safety. Even the "daredevils" among us only take calculated risks.

~*~

*Once Howard and Lois had done their bit, and since Bill and Jeanette* had no immediate plans to travel east, it was time for me to return to Newfoundland. In early June I rented a giant gas-guzzling cargo van—the largest vehicle I'd ever driven but which turned out to be surprisingly easy to handle. A whole tank of gas took me only as far as North Sydney, where I filled up again before driving aboard the ferry. The crew parked me among the eighteen-wheelers, a bare finger's width from the behemoths surrounding me. I was in the big leagues now! I swaggered a bit as I made my way to the bar for a glass of wine before trying to sleep sitting up for the third time in four months.

I slept little, instead thinking about my next steps on Mom's behalf.

Initially, we'd planned to hold a yard sale at Mom's house to clear out the last items, which would be arranged artfully throughout the rooms. We'd imagined that shoppers would come through the front door, wander around, and exit via a checkout at the back door.

The state of the floorboards on the bridge and in the rooms upstairs killed that plan. What if someone plunged through a weak spot? My imagination ran wild over broken hips and lawsuits, so it was on to Plan B.

Before leaving Nova Scotia I'd searched online for a second-hand furniture or antique dealer in Newfoundland who might be interested in the whole package. I'd called them all, but not one of them had answered the phone.

I begged Marg's husband for advice. "Try buddy out on the TCH," he said, dictating a phone number for me. "I think he's still in business." ("TCH" meant the Trans-Canada Highway.)

It took a few tries, but I finally reached Reilly, a young and eager-sounding employee of someone who seemed like an old-time rag-and-bone man.

"What do you have?" Reilly asked.

"The house has been in the same family for a hundred years," I said. "It has everything old."

"Books?"

"Yes."

"Tools?"

"Yes."

"Furniture?" Reilly's tone had risen a full octave since he'd first answered the phone.

"Yes."

"We'll have a look," Reilly said, giving me a cellphone number and a date for two days after I planned to arrive at my mother's house.

Before Reilly and his employer arrived, Marg and I began the final stages of dismantling what furniture was left in the house. Her husband arrived to help, as did Dave, his wife, and Sally's sister May with her husband.

Stains on the mattress of Mom's jury-rigged bed—likely created from a leaking hot water bottle around Mom's feet—prevented us from selling the mattress. (That, and widespread bedbug panic, which meant used mattresses were hard to even give away.) It was otherwise in good condition and it fit in the van, so I decided I would take it home with me. I left the antique headboard, pretty as it was, because I had no room for it at home.

We had always called the biggest bedroom Gramps's Room, but it was generally used as a guest room, and as Nellie's room whenever she was there. Mom had replaced a saggy old bed with a new double mattress atop a box spring on an adjustable frame. It still bothered me that Mom had purchased a whole new bed for that room because she wouldn't allow occasional guests to sleep on a saggy mattress, yet she'd allowed herself to suffer on shoeboxes every single night. But clearly no one would want to buy the double bed either, and it was far better than any mattress I had at home, so the double bed went into the van next to the twin mattress.

A narrow cot in the smallest bedroom proved to be a tiny mattress on a bench made of two-by-fours that had protruding staples on which I sliced a finger. No one wanted it, so it stayed in the house.

The large bathroom held an antique dresser, which we emptied of soap bits, rotted plastic bandages and first aid supplies, decayed rubber gloves and elastic bands, yellowed linen hand towels, and other useless items. An array of almost-empty plastic shampoo bottles—so old they had cracked—followed the dresser's contents into a garbage bag. An antique washstand appeared as if it might be of value—but it turned out to have a split down the middle of the top shelf, which Mom had disguised with a piece of cloth. The white-and-blue enamel pitcher and matching bowl that rested on the stand had been turned so the chips in the enamel faced the corner.

To Mom, if a flaw was out of sight, it didn't exist.

## CHAPTER 11

# The Turning Point

—◦—

We had finally made some headway and were getting down to the nitty-gritty of what was left in the house. Dave ultimately carted off the kitchen table for May and the gate-leg dining table and chairs for Sally. He later sent photos of them, beautifully refinished. Mom was truly pleased when I told her that May and Sally had the tables, but she still asked me once a week, "Who has the tables? I hope someone in the family has the tables."

She made the same comment about the antique sideboard, and every time she did I told her that Jackie, Marg's sister, had it.

Marg accepted the gas mower for her cottage.

We found homes for the snow tires and handed several dozen variously sized pickle jars to a neighbour, who said she would use them or find someone who could.

Several of Mom's gardening and carpentry tools and her canvas tool bag came home with me. We'd given her the bag for Christmas several years before. I had wished for one for myself, but I'd never expected I'd take home this very one—with the tags still attached.

Finally, we got to the rocks, the shells, and the driftwood.

For as long as I could remember, Mom hadn't been able go to the beach without dragging home every little thing that caught her eye. Her finds included lengths of rope, lobster traps, pebbles, shells, and giant hunks of driftwood.

Mom's pebble obsession had begun one summer when we were children. We kids were hanging upside down out of the big maple tree in front of the house when some American tourists parked their van just metres from us. It bore a bumper sticker that said, "Rockhounds."

Never shy and always curious, we demanded, "What's a rock-hound?"

They opened the back of their van to show us their treasures, which brought Mom to the front door to make sure we weren't being kidnapped. The ensuing conversation with those Americans changed her life forever. After seeing the stones they had collected and polished, and listening to their assurances that similar stones could be found right there where we lived, Mom got interested in collecting and polishing agates, which she would later turn into jewellery.

From that day forward, we never walked a beach without our heads down, searching for the dull gleam of semi-precious stones. Mom turned our dining room table into a jewellery factory, and gave us kids our first encounter with epoxy glue. At the same time, Dad and I had found a common interest in identifying Mom's rocks, and I began a collection under his guidance. While I've never had an interest in gluing steel to polished pebbles in order to wear them, I continue to collect rocks. In fact, a few years before Mom moved into The Home, I'd purchased a professional-grade tumbler to polish some of my finds.

Therefore, I wanted the rocks Mom had stashed everywhere—in the storehouse, the wood shed, and the porch. They filled bags, buckets, mugs, jars, flowerpots, bottles, and boxes, and were mixed with shells, driftwood, and—often—seaweed and stinky seawater.

I collected them all into one place and dumped everything onto an old piece of canvas that had been left over from the conveyor belt at the mill where Gramps had worked. Mom had used the belts between the rows in her garden to mulch the weeds. She pronounced the word canvas "cannavis," rhyming it with cannabis, and had no idea why we laughed every time she mentioned the cannavis in her garden!

I sorted, washed, and dried the pebbles and the most unusual shells, placing them in a large rubber tote to bring home with me. Two strong men had to lift it into the cargo van, and it had to be removed in bucket relays once I got home. It would take me a year to polish my way through less than a tenth of Mom's pebble stash. I labelled some for my collection, and—to my own surprise—made some into jewellery with twisted wire. No glue involved!

Mom had also once collected fishermen's orphaned gloves.

"They are really good gloves; I can use them in the garden," she'd say. "Look, a right one AND a left one! I don't care if they don't match!"

Howard would ask: "Did you check to see if the owner's hand is still in them? You'd better be careful."

Even after she moved into The Home, Mom continued to beachcomb as long as she could. When Howard and Lois had visited to take their turn at cleaning out the house, a norovirus was sweeping through The Home. Because Howard was a physician, and Mom had not caught the bug, she was allowed out in his company, as long as he didn't take her to any places where she could potentially spread the bug. He and Lois took her to the beach, where she found a huge piece of contorted driftwood that she insisted on taking home. They persuaded Mom there was no room at The Home, so she took it to her house so it could be artfully placed in the garden. That never happened, and it remained hidden among the tall weeds behind the woodshed long after our cleanup. I did not take it home with me!

⚓

*By the time the buy-and-sell crew arrived, we knew exactly what was to be sold and what was earmarked for family members.* Reilly, his cohort, Dicky, and their employer, Ed, ended up providing us with our funniest moments since Mom's birthday party. Reilly proved to be a gangly, geeky first-year university student who thought he'd died and gone to heaven when he laid eyes on Mom's books. He'd pick up one, read a few pages, and hug it as he carried it to a box. He repeated this procedure until the box was full, then started another box.

"I love books," he explained, misty-eyed.

*Really, Reilly?* I thought, trying not to grin too widely. He cracked me up.

Dicky had either just left his girlfriend's home or had gotten kicked out—the full story was unclear. All he wanted was a bed he could set up in the corner of Ed's garage. He said he wanted Mom's pullout couch, which was free for the taking from our point of view, but he never came to wrestle it from the living room.

Ed employed both Reilly and Dicky to pack his purchases into two '70s-era minivans, both with wired-on bumpers and mismatched fenders and doors. Ed himself was a smallish man of indeterminate age, although I later deduced he was in his eighties. He carried a cane, which he variously leaned on, used to poke potential purchases, or waved angrily at Reilly and Dicky—and he did this often. He also carried a great wad of $50 and $100 bills and a few twenties, but no tens or fives.

"Too small," he said.

When he left that first day, he peeled off three of the $100 bills to pay for the books, an antique table, two lamps, some odds and ends, and some dishes—but not many of the dishes.

"They don't sell," he said, poking through the knick-knacks. "Everyone is trying to sell their grandmother's china and crystal, and no one wants to buy it."

~·~

*I had been thinking about trying to sell Mom's crystal butter dish to Ed,* but his point about the dishes changed my mind. Besides, this was more than a butter dish: it had a story—one that might be worth more than the crystal.

It goes like this: when I was in grade four or five and we were living in Quebec, Mom hired a girl a few years older than me to help with housework. The practice of hiring a housecleaner was fairly common back then among people who could afford it. During her childhood, Mom's own mother had "help." The workers were often girls from isolated communities who had moved to town to finish school, and who helped with the housework in exchange for room and board.

Mom's intentions in hiring this girl were to give an economically disadvantaged family a leg up. We were not wealthy ourselves, but by the standards of many of our neighbours, we appeared so: we had books and toys from the Eaton's catalogue, a room for each kid, and we took summer trips to Newfoundland.

At the time, the only jewellery Mom wore was her wedding band and a Timex watch. She kept her silver cross and her engagement ring—which had an unusual stone and setting—in a jewellery box. She wore the ring only on special occasions. One day, when she went to fetch it, it was gone. Some time later, the housekeeper's mother came to visit—wearing Mom's ring. When Mom commented on the unusual piece of jewellery, the woman said her daughter had given it to her for her birthday—and wasn't it lovely? She'd never had anything so nice in her life.

Mom never said a word to the woman, but the girl was not invited back to work in our home.

My brothers and I never noticed that the ring was missing, as Mom hardly ever wore it anyway, and we didn't learn about this incident until eight or nine years later. By that time, we'd moved to a new town, and it was Mom and Dad's anniversary. In front of all of us, Dad gave Mom money and instructed her to go to a particular jeweller to buy a ring to replace her stolen engagement ring.

*Stolen?* We were agog, and insisted Mom tell us about it.

Later that day, eager to see the ring Mom had bought, I rushed home from school to catch her just as she arrived home. She looked at me a bit sheepishly. "I have to talk to your father first before I show you," she said.

*Okay, so it was going to be a romantic interlude*, I thought. I went off to do my own thing and forgot about the new ring until suppertime.

She and Dad always sat together at the dining table, across the corner from one another. When we were all seated, Dad turned to look at Mom, raised his eyebrows, and jerked his head towards the kitchen counter. That was when I noticed Mom wasn't wearing a new ring. She went and picked up a package from the counter and turned to face us all.

"Well," she began. "I tried on all the rings, and they were very nice, but they were all diamonds, and I don't want a diamond. Your father wanted me to buy a new ring, but I couldn't make up my mind. I walked around the store until I saw this."

She unwrapped the crystal butter dish.

"It's beautiful, isn't it?" she whispered. "Look how it catches the light. Better than a hundred diamonds! And it's useful and we can all share it."

Her decision made perfect sense to me.

"If your mother wants a crystal butter dish more than she wants a ring, then she should have a crystal butter dish," Dad said with his trademark grin.

We used the butter dish every day for family meals until Dad died a couple of years later. Then Mom packed it away and I never saw it again until I found it in her sideboard after she moved out.

To me, this story *is* Mom and Dad, and their relationship. It speaks of generosity, practicality, acceptance, and tolerance.

That day at Mom's I removed the butter dish from Ed's view, wrapped it, and brought it home with me. My hope is that both the story and the butter dish will find a home among Mom's descendants.

~♣~

*Meanwhile, Ed added to his growing pile: a sign made of fake wrought* iron, a couple of pictures, some frames, mugs, and other kitchen items, and two broken chairs ("Dicky will fix them"). These things went into the van. A bookcase, an old (but not antique) desk, an end table, and the broken-backed rocker followed.

Ed may have appeared eccentric—and maybe he really was—but he was also astute. He had stores in three locations in two provinces, and had a solid understanding, rooted in experience, of his customer base.

"I buy what people look for," he told me in a short and simple lesson on the business of buying and selling used items. Some people want real antiques, and they often want what's trendy, he said. But others just want something cheap and in decent shape—something they can use.

Dicky backed both patchwork vans up the hill. Marg and I pretended to pick rhubarb in the garden so we could eavesdrop on Dicky and Reilly as they bickered over how to fit their purchases into the vehicles.

"Lift your end!" commanded Dicky.

"We have to angle it sideways first," countered Reilly.

"I've been doing this longer than you. Lift your end."

"Well, you've been doing it wrong. Use your head."

"You wanna lose yours?"

And on it went. In the end, they tied the recalcitrant rocker to the roof of the minivan and drove away while we hunched behind the huge rhubarb leaves wiping away tears of laughter. Despite their general air of incompetence, Ed seemed genuinely fond of the pair and amused by the Reilly-and-Dicky show. In return, they did as he commanded.

Ed promised to return in two days to look upstairs, as well as in the storehouse and woodshed. "I'm interested in some of the other items in the house, too," he told me.

"Do you want more books?"

"No, Reilly has all he needs," Ed said, grinning like a shark. "I do, too."

Marg and I re-boxed the rest of the books, discovering that Reilly had taken most of the "literary" works, leaving a few children's books and Mom's large collection of theological tomes. I nabbed some reference books for myself and offered the theology books to the uptown church office for the use of the local clergy— two van-loads worth.

We had already quizzed family and friends about kitchen items. A teapot went to Marg's nephew, someone else wanted the portable spin washer, and a few other small items went to various friends and relatives. I brought some small and interesting china pieces home with the intention of giving them to younger family members...when I get around to it. (Actually, Mom had one of those—a round disk of wood hung on the wall, with the word "tuit" painted on it. A round tuit, of course. I didn't take it home with me.)

Marg and I took the rest of the books, bedding, and kitchen items to the Salvation Army store. "They'll lock the door if they see us coming again," I remarked as we parked in front of the store with our fourth van-load. Thankfully, this was our last.

When Ed returned, we sold him everything that was sellable. He bought the chest freezer and the big handmade wood box, both located in the back porch. When they were gone we got our first view of the layers of linoleum on the floor, right down to the original planks Gramps had nailed there in the 1900s. On top of the planks was a green fern-print linoleum that extended almost to the porch walls, and on top of that another pattern I remembered from childhood. It didn't quite cover the first layer. Next was a layer of 1970s-era gold and brown indoor–outdoor carpet that fell a hand's-width short of covering the pattern below it. On top of it all was a battleship grey linoleum, the heavy-duty kind used in schools and hospitals, that Mom had bought at a deep discount and installed in the kitchen and pantry about fifteen years earlier. Covering the porch floor with it must have been an afterthought, as it extended to just below the edge of the freezer and the woodbox.

I reflected, not for the first time, that Mom's maintenance, repairs, and interior decorating touches went as far as "what would do, would do." If no one could see it, it didn't matter.

In another episode of comic relief, Dicky and Reilly manoeuvred the full-sized refrigerator, the standard-sized clothes drier (leaving a gaping vent hole to the outdoors that we covered with chicken wire and a board), and the electric stove into the minivans and carted them off to Ed's store. Obviously, in the hands of experienced loaders, a minivan can hold a lot.

We weren't sure if we wanted to sell the big cast-iron wood stove, but no one in the family wanted it. Ed hemmed and hawed before making an acceptable offer and it was manhandled into one of the minivans for another trip.

"Take out the firebricks first," I said to Dickey. "They're heavy."

"Oh, it's ok," he said, as he and Reilly began another heated argument over how to wiggle the thing through the back door.

Someone got it into the house, I told them. I was sure they could get it out.

The stove's absence left a gaping hole in the brick chimney, which we covered with layers of black garbage bags and duct tape. We scrubbed at the stain on the fireproof base that covered the kitchen floor, successfully removing most of the discolouration. The house might be shabby, but I was determined it would be clean.

Reilly and Dicky filled the remaining gaps in the vans with small items that Ed picked from the woodshed—including some iron spikes that had once held the steel rails on which the Newfie Bullet ran, some old handsaws and bucksaws, and a bag of ancient square nails, for which Ed paid a dime apiece.

"I like to have something small for the kids to buy when they come," he said. "I'll tell them all about how the nails were made and how everything was built with them with long ago—and they'll go away with a keepsake and bit of history they'll never forget."

Sucker me—that's when I reduced the price. The vision of a 5-year-old leaving an antique shop with a treasured handmade nail got me right in the heart!

Ed wanted to buy Gramps's huge chopping block from the middle of the woodshed, but it wouldn't budge—for a very good reason. It turned out to be the actual stump of a tree, the roots buried under the floor ever since the shed had been built around it a century earlier. Mom must have inherited her MacGyver abilities from Gramps!

Ed's next trip took away headboards—including Mom's antique bed that had distressed me so profoundly—dressers, the cluttery tables and shelves, and the working ends of handle-less old garden tools. Eventually, his crew took everything except the two-by-four cot, the pullout sofa bed, some built-in shelving that refused to be removed, the curtains in the front windows, and one of history's first portable electric heaters (which I wouldn't sell in case it caused a fire in someone else's house).

With the furniture removed, I could see a big vertical wrinkle in the wallpaper on the living room wall that showed how the house had settled on either side of the stairwell and the brick chimney. Dabs of blue poster putty hung on most of the walls. The quarter-round moulding that had been nailed along the baseboard to keep flooring in place was revealed to be absent from any spot where furniture had once stood to hide it.

With the clutter gone, the voices of the past erased, and the memories removed, the house's shortcomings became obvious to even the casual eye. It was just a shabby, run-down old house, echoing with emptiness.

Barren. Hollow.

Sad.

CHAPTER 12

# *The No-Rest Home*

❧

*T*hree months after Mom moved into The Home, her house was purged and we all returned to our homes and our jobs, Mom was on her own.

At first, especially, she felt it.

"This place is a prison," she told me when I called. "I can't go anywhere and there is nothing to do in here."

"Mom, you can go anywhere you please. You can go shopping, you can visit your old friends out the mountain, you can go to the library, or to a show, or out for tea."

"I don't have a car."

"That has nothing to do with The Home. Call a cab."

"I'm not paying $25 for a cab just to go uptown."

"Why not? It's cheaper than buying a car, plus you'd have to pay for insurance and gas and registration. It's much cheaper to take a cab."

I knew she wouldn't get a car—no dealer in his or her right mind would sell a car to a deaf nonagenarian with an expired driver's licence.

Or would they?

I also knew that Mom didn't really want to go anywhere exceptional. What she wanted was to go where she wanted to go, when she wanted to go, and for as long as she wanted. "I can't even go to church," she complained.

"Yes you can. Ask Rhonda to give you a lift." Rhonda was a distant cousin who had moved into The Home several years earlier. A couple of decades younger than Mom, she still had a car and remained active at the same church.

"I don't like bugging Rhonda."

I rhymed off a list of people who passed by The Home's door on their way to church, but Mom refused to call them. "We have our little church service here on Tuesdays," she said. "I help with that. There's this retired minister here and we do the services together. He plays the music and reads some prayers and the Bible and I preach."

Mom had forgotten that I had met the retired minister a few times. He was a charming man, enormously full of himself, who enjoyed flirting with and entertaining women in his room at The Home. I didn't take to him—too flamboyant for my liking—but Mom enjoyed his company. I said nothing to her about him, even when I heard that his past included a whiff of a romantic scandal. During one visit to Mom, I couldn't locate her until a staff person suggested I knock on his door. He and Mom and his "girlfriend" (as Mom called her) were huddled together in the stifling hot room, hatching plans to escape from The Home.

"Who are you?" Mom asked suspiciously.

"Mom, it's me, Monica."

"You don't look like Monica."

I moved closer. "Oh, yes, now I see you."

She introduced me to her companions. "Come in, come in; close the door, close the door," she whispered. "We're going to break out of here. Some night soon. I'm going to Nova Scotia."

"I'm going to Bonavista," said the minister, adding that he hoped he could continue his cancer treatment in that area. "My daughter lives there, and I want to be close to my granddaughters."

"I'm moving uptown to the big home there," the girlfriend said. "The rooms are much bigger and they have more for people to do."

"You can all just walk out, you know," I told them. "Just talk to your families and they will help make arrangements. It might take a while, but it can be done and it's perfectly legal. You don't have to escape in the middle of the night."

They stared at me, eyes wide, mouths agape. Crestfallen. Obviously, they'd read one too many 1930s novels about British boarding-school pranks. I'd read a few, too, as they had been the only books worth reading at Gramps's house when I was a child.

Regretting that I'd upset their adventurous plans, I smiled and changed the subject.

"Mom, do you want to come with me to Marg's? She's cooking fish for supper."

"Oh, yes." She got off the seat of her rolling walker and turned to push it down the hall to her room, with not even a nod of goodbye to her partners-in-crime. "I don't need a walker, you know," she told me. "I just like to lean on it, and it gets people out of my way."

I did know that. I was also pleased that she wasn't too proud to use the walker, as I could foresee her true need for it in the near future. She complained often about pain in her feet and ankles, her balance was a bit off, and she was less vigorous now than she had been even a year earlier. It was, in fact, her lack of energy, combined with her stubbornness, that prevented her from organizing outings for herself, I thought. It was just too much effort. Even if Mom walked away from The Home, she likely wouldn't make it past the next intersection, so I wasn't too worried about her scheming with her buddies.

Mom never said another word about escaping, but she continued to express dissatisfaction with her situation. "There's nothing to do," was her biggest complaint. But when The Home organized two bus trips, one to a national park and another to a museum, Mom refused to go.

"I've been to the park hundreds of times," she sniffed. "And why would I want to go to that museum? Sit on a hard old bus seat for hours with a bunch of old people, just to have tea at a museum cafeteria? No way."

The buses, she found out later, were actually comfortable tour buses equipped with toilets. A fancy tea was laid on at the park and at the museum, and all who went enjoyed it. Mom was among the few residents who didn't take the trip—the others being too frail or ill. Mom later confided in Marg that she didn't want to pay for it. She hadn't understood that there was no charge for the adventure.

After that, whenever she complained about having nothing to do, I'd ask her if she was going on the next bus trip, and she would promptly change the subject. She might be forgetful, but she was too wily to forget that complaining wouldn't earn her my sympathy.

For a while she would join the regular card games in the common room, but within months her memory deteriorated to the point where she couldn't remember the rules, or which suit was trump, or, on occasion, what game they were playing. The regular card-players went along with her mistakes until a new resident joined the games and chastised Mom for making wrong moves. Mom quit, calling me to complain bitterly.

"I've been playing cards since before she was born—who does she think she is? I'm not playing with that bunch any more. I'm moving to Nova Scotia."

"I'm moving to Nova Scotia" became Mom's default plan when anything went wrong. If she started a conversation with this statement, I knew she'd been challenged or criticized, and I knew she wasn't getting her own way.

"What's up?" I'd ask, to hear a litany of woes, ranging from the completely ridiculous to the worrisome.

There was the time she refused to take a bath or a shower for a couple of weeks. The bathing rooms weren't clean, she said, and she could just take a sponge bath at the sink in her room. A concerted effort by Auntie H., Howard and Lois, Marg, me, and the staff persuaded her that The Home's bathtubs were cleaner than she was, and that she'd get sick and stinky if she didn't bathe.

On another occasion, Mom accidentally lowered her venetian blind onto the back of her own head, causing a small bump. Blinds, like computers, always defeated Mom. At any house where we'd had those blinds, she'd left them either all the way up or all the way down. At The Home, she ignored the blind in favour of a towel strung across the bottom half of the window at night. Mom's ingenuity at work again!

"Someone could see right in," she complained to me—as if anyone would want to look. But I did understand her concern. I didn't know until some time later that every day the cleaning staff took down her towel, and every night Mom put it right back up. Finally, The Home replaced her blind with café-style curtains.

"My dear, they're lovely," Mom enthused. "The girls here are so good!"

She continued to hoard newspapers, with the staff gently culling them from the bottom of the pile so as not to initiate a confrontation. At the beginning of her second year, the newspaper changed from a daily paper with a paid subscription to a weekly flyer—free. God knows how many of these she collected from the front lobby.

Periodically Mom complained about the food, but she refused to eat at a restaurant even when she had the opportunity. "Why would I? I have a perfectly good meal waiting for me in the dining room."

For the same reason, she refused all invitations to go to a café uptown for tea. The Home served biscuits and tea every afternoon, and if Mom was already paying for it, she was determined not to miss it. She would accept an invitation to someone's house, though; afternoon tea was free at Marg's or Auntie H.'s, so she wasn't paying twice.

Mom pocketed food items from the dining room, storing them in her small refrigerator until they were no longer fit to eat. Regular visitors soon learned to simply remove any food that had turned without trying to argue with Mom over it. If she hadn't remembered to eat it, she wasn't going to miss it.

"Monica, do you know where I stashed my money?" she asked when I called her one day about a year after her move. "I can't find my money."

"Which money is that?"

"I had money here in my room, but I can't find it."

Visions of light-fingered staff flashed through my mind until I remembered the money I'd found stashed in the house. "I found money hidden in your house when we cleaned it," I said. "I used it to pay for your table and your fridge and some other things."

"No, this is money I had the other day."

"The other day" could mean any day at all, and until that point I'd seen no activity on her bank account.

"Did you take it out of your bank account?"

"Nooo...I had it for a while."

"Maybe you spent it and forgot," I suggested.

"Maybe."

"You can go to the bank any time and take out money, you know. Just don't take too much out at once, and don't flash it around. Somebody might try to steal it."

"No one here would do that!"

"Well, someone might forget whose room they're in, or they might even forget that they're not supposed to do that. I expect there are some forgetful people at The Home."

"There certainly are," Mom agreed, and went on to describe her neighbours' acts of forgetfulness. "Poor things. I can't blame them. I'm just happy it's not me."

I smothered a giggle.

"How am I going to get to the bank?" she demanded.

"Your sister always wants to take you out to places. Get her to stop at the bank. And then you can take her for tea."

So she did—and she actually took Auntie H. for tea. She said nothing about it to me, though. I happened to notice the withdrawal during my regular check on Mom's accounts. Auntie H. called me afterward to express her surprise at Mom's sudden urge to treat her. She'd believed Mom's claims that she had no money to spare.

"Mom has enough money," I replied.

In the same vein, Mom still appeared reluctant to make long-distance calls, even though she had a package that covered Canada-wide calls.

"Have you been talking to Nellie?"

"That's long-distance."

"It's already paid for, Mom. You can call Nellie as often as you like and it won't cost you anything."

"Oh, okay. I didn't know that."

She'd been told—often—but she'd forgotten.

A few days later, she'd tell me all Nellie's news, and then there would be silence on the subject for another few months, until I'd remind her that she could call Nellie for free.

Meanwhile, Nellie would occasionally call me for a chat, and to check up on Mom. While Nellie suffered from poor physical health, mentally she was sharper than Mom—and thus able to grieve for Mom's loss of memory.

"Oh, my dear," she'd begin. "Your poor mother—when I think of how smart she always was, able to do whatever she wanted, and now look at her. It breaks my heart."

After six months at the home, Mom's confusion and forget-fulness were becoming even more obvious. Often, she didn't know what day it was, couldn't remember names of people she knew well, and forgot where she had put things. She spoke of The Home's dining room as being downstairs, but the facility was all on one floor. She would swear on a stack of Bibles that no one had been to visit her in months but I generally knew otherwise.

As time went on, though, she became more accustomed to her room and the facility. She was rarely late for meals and was happy to hold lengthy conversations with other residents, even when she had no idea who they were! Luckily, she forgot that she couldn't remember, and so did her friends—so all was well.

~·~

*Mom's strange obsessions and impulses were another matter. The most* concerning issue during her first year at The Home was a fixation on another resident, a woman a good dozen years older. Mom was convinced that this centenarian was not being well cared for.

"Aggie's family never visits her," she said angrily.

I knew they did visit, using a back entrance near Aggie's room and out of Mom's sight.

"They just come in once in a while and stuff things in her fridge and leave!" Mom said. "She doesn't want food. She wants their company."

After a few attempts to persuade Mom that Aggie's family treated her fine, I gave up. I knew from mutual acquaintances that Aggie's family members were reasonably well off. They'd decided against winter vacations in order to spend time with their mother, and they loved her and did visit her.

I also knew that, rather than see Aggie go into a hospital to die alone behind a curtain when the time came, her family had asked that she be allowed to stay at The Home where she could pass away peacefully among friends. The Home was mostly designed for able-bodied residents who needed little care, but Aggie had stayed on as she aged. For her, dying at The Home would be dying at home because she'd lived there for so long.

Aggie required little extra care, as it happened. Every day, she got herself out of bed and dressed herself. But if she got sick, or if she didn't show up for breakfast, Mom would go and sit with her. Then Mom began to try to nurse Aggie, hovering over her at all hours, and making slight interventions that did nothing to improve the old woman's health. Mom just wanted to look after someone, and had the best of intentions—long known as the pavement on the road to hell.

Mom would wipe away what she thought was pus oozing around Aggie's eyes, but it was actually ointment that had been prescribed by the doctor. When she was told by the nurse to leave Aggie's eyes alone, Mom took a chair to the hallway outside Aggie's room and sat there until the wee hours of the morning. The staff wisely left her alone until she gave up her vigil and took herself to bed.

The next morning, Mom was too sick to go to breakfast. She was more likely too stubborn, I thought, when I heard about it. The staff cheerfully ignored Mom's drama and left her in bed. She eventually got up for lunch.

Before long she was back at Aggie's door, waking her up to give her tea, helping her out of bed to go to the bathroom, and taking on other tasks that belonged to the nursing staff. When the RN scolded her, Mom lashed out, telling her she knew all about nursing and that the nurses at The Home knew nothing.

It wasn't even remotely true. Mom had taken a St. John Ambulance first aid and home nursing course when she'd attended college in Toronto—seventy years earlier. That was the extent of her nursing training.

Filled with righteous indignation, Mom went back to her own room and called the health-care authorities to report that The Home wasn't looking after Aggie. Under the law, any report has to be investigated, so the authorities had to take Mom's accusations seriously. Though the claim was unfounded, and eventually The Home received a positive report, an investigative visit from a health inspector was bad optics.

That was the first time the owners called me to try to stop Mom from interfering in Aggie's care. We discussed ways and means, finally deciding that a series of distractions would be the best way to steer Mom toward other fascinations. We discussed things like involving her in other residents' problems (since she seemed to like to fix things), or getting her outdoors to blow off some steam, or possibly putting electronic monitors on Aggie's door and Mom's key fob to alert the desk if Mom went into Aggie's room.

While I was still looking into that last option, Mom called to complain angrily that everyone was talking about her behind her back.

*They'd have good reason*, I thought, but I didn't say it out loud.

"What do you mean, Mom?"

"I hear them talking," she said. "They're out in the hall, right outside my door. Sometimes I can hear them whispering about me in the next room."

"Hmm." My mind buzzed with the fact that Mom could barely hear her television with the volume as high as it would go. How could she possibly hear anyone talking about her, let alone if they were whispering?

"How do you know they were talking about you?"

"They said my name."

"How often has this happened?"

"Once, that I remember."

*Really.*

"Maybe one of them was calling the other about cleaning your room or bringing fresh towels or something."

"Uh...no. I don't think so." She was less sure.

"Or maybe it was the television in the next room. Or maybe one of the other residents asking if you were in."

"Well, maybe."

"Those girls are too professional to talk about a resident outside their door, Mom. They just wouldn't do it."

I changed the subject, but Mom's call made it clear to me that she was more than just forgetful. I might be able to add delusional and paranoid to the list. If her condition was worse than we'd all initially believed, she might have to move to a facility that offered closer supervision. She wouldn't like that.

A day or two later, I thought I'd have to pack her up and move Mom again when staff members found Aggie's oxygen tubes in a tangle on her dresser, right after Mom had left the room. This was no longer simple busybody activity—it was placing someone's life in danger.

I read Mom the riot act.

"If Aggie had died, you'd be charged with murder," I scolded. "If you see someone having problems, call the nurse. It's not your job to look after people. You have to stop interfering or they'll transfer you to a secure unit like The Lodge."

The Lodge accommodated people with serious dementia, including those who were violent. Mom might not see herself that way, but if she was unable to follow protocols and she endangered the safety of others, The Lodge was a definite option. I worried over it and then spoke to The Home's administrator.

"Oh, my dear, she's fine," the woman soothed me. "We can handle it. Your mom is not ready for any kind of heavier care."

Instead of blaming Mom, she laid down the law to all residents: no one was to touch another person's oxygen tubes, to give anyone rides on their four-wheeled walkers (one of Mom's favourite bits of recreation), or to hand out meds.

Mom balked at these new restrictions. "I want to go to Nova Scotia," she said, meaning that she wanted to be moved to a seniors' facility here.

"Okay," I said—again. "It will take a few years but I can start the ball rolling. Where would you like to go?"

"The one near you that we visited the last time I was there." Mom was way past being able to function at that particular facility—she needed more care than they could provide—but I didn't tell her that.

She continued to fuss over Aggie until even Aggie got annoyed. Whether they had words, I don't know, but Mom suddenly shifted her focus to a man with sore legs who apparently wanted Mom to rub salve on them. (Sure he did.) Then there was a woman who followed Mom to her room every morning after breakfast in order to nap in Mom's bed while Mom sat in her recliner reading the paper. Another woman, who (according to Mom) wanted to talk all the time, followed her around constantly, and there was also a man she occasionally joined on a bench outdoors to admire the weather and talk politics. I heard little more about Aggie, and nothing more about the minister and his girlfriend.

Truthfully, I was scared to ask Mom about any one of them, in case it started her off again. Mom stopped saying she wanted to move to Nova Scotia—which was fine, because I'd lied. I'd never "started the ball rolling."

~ ⚜ ~

*It had not escaped me that Mom might think I had done what she'd ac-cused* Aggie's family of doing: dumping her in The Home, cleaning out her house, and then returning to Nova Scotia to ignore her from afar. I could feel her disapproval in my bones. Before she moved, I'd called her every morning, but afterward I called her just once or twice a week. Spacing the calls was a deliberate tactic at first, designed to keep Mom from waiting for my calls instead of enjoying The Home's social life. It was a relief for me to sleep past 7:30 every morning after years of rotating my life around my daily call.

Now, whenever I thought of calling her, I'd check the clock to see if she'd likely be in her room. During the first month, she answered all my calls on the first ring. After she'd lived there for a while, I'd have to leave a message on the answering machine, although I was pretty sure she didn't know how to access her mes-sages. If I couldn't reach her for more than a week, I'd call The Home's office to find out if she was all right. She always was, but on occasion someone would check her phone for me to see if she'd hung it up properly. Invariably, the line was still open or the phone wasn't charged.

I was also pretty sure Mom couldn't remember when I'd called last anyway, because she didn't remember her other calls. For in-stance, Howard would tell me he'd been chatting with her, but when I'd ask her the next day if she'd heard from him, she'd say, "No, not in quite a while." The upside of this was that if she complained her family was ignoring her, we knew it wasn't true!

I started sharing this insight with friends of mine in similar situations, and their relief was palpable. "Just don't stop calling," I advised.

## CHAPTER 13

# *Journey to Contentment*

~•~

*M*om *finally began to enjoy herself around the time of her first* Christmas at The Home.

By then, her sister had gone south, my brothers and I had retreated to our various homes, her nephews and nieces and their extended families had finished their summer vacations in Newfoundland and had gone back to their jobs and schools elsewhere, and intermittent snowfalls threatened easy travel. It was sink or swim for Mom. No one was around to distract her from her woes— real or imagined.

So when I called her one Sunday afternoon in mid-December, I expected to hear a litany of her usual complaints about The Home. Instead, I heard: "I can't talk, Monica. They're having a party in the lounge and I have to go." And she hung up—without even a goodbye.

That evening she called me back to describe the party. It had included live music by a man from "out the bay." There had been dancing, a Santa Claus, a plenty of treats and gifts.

"This is such a wonderful place," Mom enthused. "The people here are so good!"

I agreed heartily, and listened to her repeat the details about the party twice more.

"Hallelujah!" I breathed when I hung up forty-five minutes later.

Some weeks earlier I had begun replying to the Christmas cards that Canada Post had forwarded to me from Mom's house. I told the senders she'd moved and I gave them her phone number and new address. I promised to forward their cards to Mom, adding that she would love to hear from them or see them if they happened to be in her neighbourhood.

Quite a number of her old friends called me to ask after Mom, and several—to her immense delight—did visit her, including a former Member of Parliament who had been one of her students, some distant cousins from Labrador, and some former work colleagues from the college.

"How did they know I was here?" she asked, her surprise audible.

"I told them, Mom."

"My dear, it was lovely to see them all," she said. "I want you to send me all their addresses so I can keep in touch." I agreed, even though she already had them—I'd included a list of names and addresses in each package of cards I'd sent her.

Every time I called that winter, she described the beauty outside her window: the sun on the snow, the deep green trees, the colour of the sky—always adding how happy she was that she didn't have to shovel. As winter wound into spring, Mom told me she wanted to move back into her house for the summer so Nellie could visit.

"Oh, Mom, you can't," I said. "The water is turned off, all the beds are gone, the stove is gone; everything is gone. The toilet is broken. The house is empty and it's for sale."

A relative had earlier put me in contact with a realtor friend in Ontario who'd offered to help with the sale of the house. I'd contacted the friend, who, in turn, had put me in touch with Lenny, his Newfoundland colleague. Lenny had come to look at the house when we were still clearing it out; once it was empty, we had put it on the market.

"We might as well sell it then."

Sigh.

"Good idea, Mom. We'll do that."

"Maybe Nellie can stay with Marg."

As much as Mom wanted and expected Nellie to visit her in Newfoundland, I explained to her that it wasn't going to happen. Persistent lesions on Nellie's feet and legs, as well as worsening emphysema, kept her housebound in Montreal with regular nursing care. If they were going to see each other face-to-face, Mom would have to visit her. My mind raced through the logistics of getting Mom to Nellie's.

"Do I have enough money to go?"

"You sure do."

"Well, can you book me a Gulf crossing and my bus ticket?"

"Mom, you are not going to Montreal by bus."

"Why not? I can do it."

Oh, me nerves.

Instead of succumbing to the urge to shout, "No you can't!" I replied, "It's too tiring for you, and you might get sick like you did after your birthday. Remember?"

"I wasn't sick."

*Change the direction of the conversation*, I remembered.

"We'll fly, and I'll go with you. Just us girls."

"Oh, would you? That would be lovely! When?"

I took a quick glance at the desk calendar.

"Around the end of April."

"That's a long way off."

"It's only a few weeks, and it will take that long to organize everything. Besides, the weather will be better."

"That's true. You'll look after it?"

"I will look after it."

I did—which turned out to be another elephantine project. The first order of business was to find out whether Mom was healthy enough to travel, which, it turns out, she was. Aside from a little swelling in her feet, the doctor declared her fit. In fact, Marg told me, after a visit to Mom that involved them both trotting around The Home's outdoor pathways, "My dear, she could walk to Montreal!"

Normally, I would book flights without the help of a travel agent, but at this point my life was too busy. The agency with the best-looking ad in the phone book got the job.

It would be a gruelling journey: a late-evening flight from Halifax to Newfoundland for me, followed by a day of packing Mom's suitcase and making sure she had her meds and photo ID, then an early morning two-stage trip to Montreal with a flight change in Halifax. After five days we'd fly back to Newfoundland, again with a stop in Halifax to change planes. I would settle Mom into The Home for the night and, within hours, board a predawn flight back to Nova Scotia.

Marg offered me a bed for my two overnights in Newfoundland, and Nellie's niece, Bess, invited me to stay with her in Montreal. Mom would stay with Nellie at her assisted living apartment.

As we all know, even the best-laid plans can go awry. Melting snow and rainfall of Biblical proportions left several areas around Montreal flooded in the weeks before our departure. Television images implied that the whole island of Montreal was under water.

"Don't worry," Bess told me. "We're not affected."

When Mom suggested in one of her rare calls to me that perhaps we should cancel the trip, I was ready with the promise that we would be on dry land. We would probably be able to walk everywhere in sandals, I told her.

"Hmmph."

"Getting cold feet?" I teased.

"A little. You know I hate flying."

"Well, you'll just have to wear warm socks in your sandals," I told her firmly. "The tickets are bought. We're going."

Then came the next obstacle: a few days before our departure, Bess called to say that Nellie was sick with both pneumonia and influenza. She was in hospital, hooked to a forest of tubes, IVs, and monitors. Bess thought Nellie should be out of hospital by the time we got there, but suggested it would be better if both Mom and I stayed with her rather than risk catching whatever bug Nellie was carrying. I hesitated before agreeing, thinking of the extra work for Bess.

I soon realized that staying with Bess should have been Plan A. As the trip progressed, it became increasingly obvious that Mom couldn't look after herself. Mom had promised she could walk between airport gates in Halifax, but her unsteady gait prompted me to nab a wheelchair and an attendant to push it. Without it, we would have missed our connecting flight.

Mom never knew where she was, even when I'd told her just moments before, nor was she sure of her destination. From the beginning, I took possession of her identification and tickets, which prevented us from being stranded at security as we left Newfoundland—where she'd had to endure the apparent indignity of having her suitcase examined. The batteries in her ever-present flashlight had attracted the attention of airport security. Once past that obstacle, we boarded the plane.

"We're not going overseas, are we?"

"Just over the Cabot Strait, Mom."

"This is rather a nice bus," Mom commented, looking around.

At a later point in the trip, flying over northern New Brunswick, Mom commented on a mountain she could see through the window. I couldn't imagine a mountain in that area that would have been tall enough to pierce the cloud cover. I leaned across her to peer down.

"There," Mom said, jabbing a finger. I followed her line of sight. She was pointing to a triangular bracket on the airplane's wing, the type used to fasten a safety harness during maintenance. When I explained what it was, she actually understood. A few minutes later she commented on the strange shade of blue in a part of the sky. It turned out she was looking at another part of the wing!

I wished I had someone with me to share the humour in that moment.

In Montreal, we went straight to the hospital, where Nellie remained in the pulmonary unit, attached to all the bells and whistles. She was in an isolation room where all visitors had to gown, glove, and mask before entering; if we had to leave—even for a short trip to the washroom or to get a drink—we had to shed the protective gear and wash our hands, then wash again and don new gowns, gloves, and masks to re-enter the room. Mom's hospital-visiting experience allowed her to easily accept the hoses and tubes connected to Nellie. The Personal Protective Equipment was a different story. We had to remind her to stop pushing the plastic shield upwards, to keep the mask over her nose, and to keep the gloves on her hands.

As soon as we walked out the hospital doors after a lengthy visit, Mom forgot that Nellie was in the hospital. When we arrived at Bess's home, Mom asked when she could see Nellie.

"Tomorrow," I said.

Then she suggested that she return to The Home to sleep that night, and was surprised to hear that she was in Montreal.

"Oh, wonderful," she crowed. "I can go visit Nellie!"

"Yes, Mom, you certainly can. We'll go tomorrow."

Bess and her husband had moved a bed into their dining room for Mom and had made up a cot for me in the living room across the hall. Several times through the night Mom wandered into the living room looking for the bathroom, which was a few metres away in the opposite direction. I got up each time to show her the way, and returned to my cot to lie awake until I heard her coming back.

After one such trip, though, she didn't come back. Instead, she stopped at a different entrance to the living room and stood looking around in the dark. By the time I realized where she was and rolled out of my cot to get her, she'd curled up on the cold leather couch. She crossly refused to move to her bed.

"Leave me alone, Monica!"

I did, but first I gathered her comforter from the dining room and tucked it around her.

After a few sleepless hours on my part, I heard her voice. "What are you doing here in my room, Monica?"

"You're in my room."

---

## *Memory Loss*

Memory loss affects 40 percent of people over the age of 65. If there is no underlying medical reason, it can be a normal part of aging.

**Signs of age-related memory loss in a loved one:**

- They forget a conversation or event from a year ago.
- They forget an acquaintance's name.
- They occasionally forget things and events.
- They sometimes can't find a word.

Dementias like Alzheimer's disease are different from age-related memory loss. If you are concerned about your memory, consult your doctor.

**Signs of dementia in a loved one:**

- They can't recall recent events or conversations.
- They don't recognize family members or remember their names.
- They frequently forget things or events.
- They frequently pause or substitute words when speaking.
- People close to them worry about their memory, but they see no problem.

(Not a diagnostic tool. Source: Alzheimer Society of Canada.)

After a lot of persuasion, she moved into her warm bed. "This isn't the same bed I was told to sleep in," she said.

"Actually, it is," I said—ignoring all advice against arguing with her.

"I don't think so," she said, but she pulled up the blankets and slept—waking up every half hour to sigh loudly or proclaim, "Oh my, oh my, oh my!"

At one point during the night I awakened to see her wandering in front of me like a lost, squat ghost, a white towel held like an offering, high in her open hand, palm up. She wore nothing but a white silk pyjama top that flapped around her pale bare legs, scarcely covering a droopy Depends.

Try as I might, I still can't un-see that image of a lost, confused, paranoid, deaf, obsessive, demented, forgetful old woman. She was still my dear, sweet Mom, though. As my kids are fond of saying, "It is what it is."

I guided her back to her bed and heard nothing more from her for several hours.

~*~

*All of Mom's behaviour was normal for someone with memory loss, but* until that visit I had not appreciated how much her recall had failed, or how her other cognitive abilities had been affected. The trip put to rest my lingering guilt about having moved Mom to The Home instead of having her live with any of us or in her own home, even with a team of caregivers.

When Mom got back to The Home after our trip she couldn't wait to get into her room. Although we arrived late, the night staff person was ready for her, greeting her warmly. Mom was incredibly

delighted to see him, and he responded in kind. Once Mom was
settled and I started for the door, he followed me—to lock the
exterior door, I assumed.

But in fact he wanted to share a few words of wisdom. Maybe
he was worried I was jealous of Mom's effusive greeting to him,
or that I was disappointed she was so happy to part from me. Or
maybe he thought I was sad about leaving her. Whatever his motive,
I appreciated his words.

"They're all like that after they've been here a little while," he
told me. "They are just so happy to be home, and they do see this
as their home."

I don't remember what I said in reply, but I believed him to
my core, and I was deeply moved that he understood my feelings—
perhaps better than I did.

It was true. Anyone who took Mom out to dinner or to church
or a family gathering reported that when she got tired, she wanted
to go "home." Even events within The Home saw her retiring to
her room and closing the door. Safety, privacy, rest, a sense of be-
longing, and the knowledge that her family was a mere phone call
away—it all began to sound pretty attractive, even to me!

I remember a moment from years ago, when I was a cub
reporter at a community newspaper. The editor often assigned me
to cover stories about nursing home residents who had formed a
choir, adopted a cat, made pickles in the facility's kitchen, or done
something else of interest to families and friends on the "outside."
On one occasion, when I'd pressed the buzzer to be admitted, I
saw a man in a wheelchair who had parked himself in the sunny
vestibule between the lounge and the main door. His eyes were
closed, and his hands were clasped over a book spread open on

the multicoloured afghan that covered his lap. He was the picture of contentment.

*When I get old, that's what I want,* I'd thought at the time. *A sunny spot to sit with my book.* There would be no one asking me to do something, no worries about meals or washing dishes or shovelling snow, no wondering whether the dog was in or out, or if the doors were locked. I would sit and think, to make up for all the times I'd never had the chance.

So I understood the appeal for Mom to get home to what had become her "own little room" and her "own little bed," terms she'd often used during my childhood to express her joy in coming home. How often over the past twenty-five years had she returned to her empty house after travelling to find it drab and cold and lonely? Or had she rejoiced in her familiar surroundings? She'd never complained.

A funny thing, the concept of home. More than a year after moving, Mom had finally begun to call her room at The Home "home" and her home out around the bend in the road "the house."

~⋆~

*The realtor and I had kept in touch by email, and had arranged to sign* all contracts and agreements digitally. My grandfather would have been amazed to see such a thing, I mused. Gramps was considered a forward-thinking man for his time, having lived and worked in the Yankee States, and having brought the wonders of that world back to Newfoundland with him.

He'd built his house with his bare hands—cut and milled and sawed every timber and sash and moulding. That was typical of the men of his time and place, but Gramps had gone further. He'd installed the community's first indoor plumbing, which involved making a septic tank from two big rum puncheons. The system lasted until the introduction of a city sewage collection system in the mid-1960s. He'd also brought in a generator and wired the house for electricity—unimaginable to the neighbours at the time. Most of the original wiring was still there when Mom moved into the house, and she'd simply had circuits added to it, which explains why there were never enough outlets for all her appliances or electronics.

As modern as Gramps had been as a young man, when the Apollo astronauts walked on the moon in July 1969, he'd refused to believe it had actually happened. We were with him for our annual vacation at the time, and he'd bought a little television so we could watch the event together. Despite seeing it on the screen, he wouldn't accept that the broadcast was real, or even that the events were possible.

"They just made that up in Hollywood," he scolded as he watched. "Don't believe a word of it, my duckies!" His was the first conspiracy theory I ever heard on the topic, but it wasn't the last. No doubt if he could have seen the internet at work, he'd have been gobsmacked.

But while Mom was finally settled, her affairs were decidedly not. Her house was still not sold. My repeated calls to the agent's office weren't answered; finally I called his cellphone.

"I've never seen the housing market this flat," Lenny said. "It's terrible." He had proposed that the market was likely to spike around Christmas.

"It's like this," I told him. "The longer that house sits empty, the worse it is going to get. In another year, it may need a new roof or new windows. The longer it sits, the more municipal taxes I have to pay, and the more insurance, too."

Lenny saw my point. We had lowered the price early that summer by more than $20,000, but it still hadn't moved. No one had even come to look at it.

Mom suggested we change real estate agents. "I don't think this one is very good. I don't think he is trying hard enough."

I explained again that the market right now was slow—many Newfoundlanders working in the Alberta oil patch had lost their jobs, and there were a lot of homes for sale. I had a contract with the agent, I added, and said he must be reasonably good because he was in charge of a large region.

"Then he's probably too busy to bother trying to sell my house," Mom snapped. "He'd be more interested in the mansions up the Humber." This was a reference to the fact that, a couple of decades earlier, wealthy Europeans had built impressively large homes near the Humber River, commuting through the local airport to ski, fish, and hunt in Newfoundland. Subsequent airline schedule changes had made the commute more difficult, which prompted many of the owners to put their houses on the market and stay home in Germany or Norway or wherever they were from. There was no denying that Mom's house was not on a scale with the grand Humber homes, but it was affordable. If the new owner was handy at all, my mother's house was a steal—even with the necessary repairs.

But as the seasons passed, Mom grew more worried. "I wonder if we should hire someone to tar the roof," she said, on one of the rare occasions when she called me. "If the roofing comes off, the whole house will be ruined."

"We'll see," I replied. By that time, I was resigned to the new owner tearing down the building, so why replace the roof?

In another phone conversation Mom suggested we lower the price yet again. That was fine with me. I wanted the house off my plate and out of my midnight anxieties. I contacted Lennie and he dropped the price by another $10,000. I really hoped—fingers crossed, prayers going up and all that—that someone would notice the discount and seal the deal. Handling Mom's affairs would be a lot easier if all her assets were in one place: the bank.

Then the veranda fell off. The real estate agent emailed to say he'd taken prospective buyers to the view the property only to find that the weight of the snow had buckled the veranda's supports, pulling the deck away from the 1970s aluminum siding; the whole thing had collapsed inward against the house.

Since Lenny had his "special agent lock" (as I called it) on the front door, he had to clamber over the mess to open the house and let the visitors in through the back door. No doubt the people had been attracted by the low price despite the challenge of repairs. But the collapsed veranda put an end to their interest.

Lenny blocked access to the mess with a sawhorse and some yellow tape and called me.

"It's not worth rebuilding," I replied, before realizing I should consult my brothers. "I'll call you back."

Tear it right off and lower the price to cover the cost of building a new deck, said my brothers. That was easy to say, but try finding someone to do it! Our once–vigorous-and-reliable handypeople, as with any aging population, now had sore backs and aching limbs and didn't want to risk their chainsaws cutting old nail-filled timbers. I was willing to pay, but I'd hoped the job would be more attractive to someone looking to salvage a bit of firewood; turns out no one had any use for whatever firewood might be recovered in the process. The all-around verdict was that the wood would likely have to go to the dump.

Mom had considered replacing the bridge a few years earlier but had changed her mind when she'd discovered it would cost thousands of dollars. It took me a couple of days, but I was able to track down the fellow—Brian—who'd given her that estimate. He offered to remove the broken bridge now for a reasonable fee, and to get rid of the debris either in his workshop furnace or in the landfill. Sweet relief.

～∗～

*My mother's house had always seemed to be in reasonable enough shape* while she had lived there, if one didn't look too closely. Once it was empty and bare, its shortcomings were all too obvious, and things were just getting worse with each passing season.

Mom had replaced the roof twenty years earlier, but the shingles had peeled away, waiting for a good storm to rip them off entirely. The century-old window frames were fragile, in some places held together by putty and paint and protected only by the aluminum storm windows Mom had installed. We had been confident that those issues, along with the required plumbing and electrical work, could have been addressed by a determined do-it-yourselfer—if they had been able to get their hands on the place before too much more time had passed.

But now too much time had passed. "It might be a tear-down," Lenny sighed.

If so, that was fine. None of us was blind to the house's deficiencies, nor were we attached to the place as our ancestral home. But it would still be easier to sell it whole and let new owners make the decisions about demolition.

Early on, Dave had proposed contacting a friend of a friend who'd created a sideline business dismantling old-fashioned Newfoundland homes; he would fill a tractor-trailer with rustic bits and pieces and haul it all to Montreal or Toronto to sell to rich people who wanted the "country" look, but without the country living. Dave figured our grandfather's handmade mouldings and wainscoting, the antique locks and hardware, and the watery old window glass might fit the bill.

But when Dave reached out to him after the veranda caved, he discovered that the salvage guy had found a "real job" and was no longer scavenging old houses.

We had a dilemma on our hands. In order to look after the interests of "heirs and successors," should we spend the money to make repairs? Or should we just spend the money to tear down the building and sell the property? Or should we simply lower the price and sell the house "as is?"

Bill was still optimistic. "It's a great place for someone from Newfoundland living away who wants a place to stay when they come home for vacations. All they need to do is fix it up enough to be reasonably comfortable as a cottage. They can pick away at other repairs and renos as they go."

Howard agreed. "It will sell," he stated with confidence.

I hoped they were right. The price was attractively low, and we were selling the house and the land together for little more than the price of an empty lot without city services.

Meanwhile, taxes, insurance, and electricity bills had to be paid, and someone had to keep an eye on the place. It was a blessing that Mom had good neighbours, and that the real estate agent was helpful above and beyond the call of duty.

Over the next year, I was haunted nightly by the possibility that a homeless person might break in to find a place to sleep and then accidentally burn the place down or fall down the stairs and die.

Then the COVID-19 quarantine flatlined the real estate business, while the tax, insurance, and power bills kept coming in. Even Mom began worrying about the cost of keeping the house with no one in it, to the point of suggesting at least once a week that she should move back in. Knowing I couldn't face another year stressing over my mother's house, I consulted my brothers again about tearing the whole thing down.

We figured demolition would cost about $10,000, and without a house, the value of the property would go down by at least that much again—which totalled a bit less than what it would cost to pay the bills for another year.

We had finally made up our minds to do it. Dave suggested I ask Brian, the fellow who'd taken down the collapsed veranda, to do the job. If he didn't want to do it, he'd likely know someone who would.

As fate would have it, Brian was interested in the property himself. He made a reasonable offer, subtracting the $10,000 demolition cost, because he was going to do it himself.

Two years and three months after Mom moved out, the deal was finally sealed.

"The house is sold," I told Mom.

"What's he going to do with it? Fix it up? Make apartments?"

Wisely, I think, we had decided not to tell her the plan. "Once it's his, he can do what he likes," I said. "He likes the gardens, especially the rhubarb and the raspberry patches, and he loves the view. I think he'll treat the property with respect."

"I want you to take some of the house money and send a bit to every person in the family," Mom instructed.

And when all was said and done, that's exactly what I did.

## CHAPTER 14

# Mom and Her Money

❦

*B*y *forcing myself to remember more details about the days when we* were all kids living at home with our parents, I realized that Mom had never been a great housekeeper. Dust bunnies had multiplied under the beds like rabbits. One day's dishes were quite often stacked in the sink on top of those from the day before. Kids and dogs and cats and hamsters ran roughshod, leaving muddy footprints, hair, and other detritus in every corner.

But the enormity of the semi-squalor in which Mom had lived in her latter years haunts me still. Although she wasn't wealthy, Mom could easily have afforded the kind of live-in help that would have allowed her to stay in her home for the rest of her life. She also had the funds to make the necessary repairs to the house—the roof, the hot water heater, the deck, the rotten window frame. And she could have renovated the ground floor to include a bathroom and bedroom for her old age. But she hadn't done these things, and had never even seriously considered doing any of it. Why not?

My guess is that she didn't have a strong understanding of her actual financial circumstances. It had been a family joke that Mom was never good at math, but none of us had ever imagined that she couldn't count money. My brothers and I had always believed her refusal to spend was because she didn't have enough, rather than because she didn't know how much she had. But did she truly not understand that she had money, or was she simply scared to divulge how much she had in case someone took advantage of her?

If she believed she was poor, she could have asked her bank's financial advisor to walk her through her future needs and her capacity to pay for them. She could have talked to one of my brothers or me, or to the woman who did her taxes. It seemed unlikely that she thought we would take advantage of her, as she often offered us—her children—money without us asking. Every time she spent money on us, we worried that her generosity would leave her short, so we tried to curtail those expenditures without hurting her feelings. On the few occasions we borrowed from her, we paid it back with interest—but she may not have realized it.

We had never asked Mom about her finances for fear of arousing her suspicions about our motives for asking—we knew how her mind worked! Decades of her regaling us with stories of horrible families who'd fleeced their parents of all their money and shoved them into nursing homes had had their effect. Indeed, a bit of research proved that families are not the only ones who take advantage of seniors. Government agencies designated as guardians have sent people they've rarely or never met into care homes after deeming them incapable—with minimal evidence of their diminished needs and abilities. Such appointed guardians have been known to "lose" their clients' assets, make poor financial decisions on their behalf, and fail to properly protect them. So Mom's fears were not completely baseless.

But Mom actually had money.

By the time she moved into The Home, Mom had lived so frugally that she still had her entire nest egg. Howard and I had vowed that we would make sure her money was used for her care and not saved as an inheritance for her offspring.

Not long after she'd moved into The Home, Mom had gotten into a discussion with some residents whose only income was Old Age Security and Canada Pension. They'd described how most of their money went toward their accommodation and meals at The Home, leaving them with little to spend. They'd schemed about a way to disguise their income and told Mom she should do the same. Mom's case was entirely different, because she was paying out of her own pocket, but she didn't understand that. She called me in a panic, saying she didn't have any money because it was all going to The Home for her keep. What was she going to do?

I felt like saying that even if The Home took every penny she had, it wouldn't matter, because she didn't want to spend anything anyway—but I didn't.

"You have enough money," I told her.

"I do? How much do I have?"

I gave her a ballpark figure and she perked up right away.

"Oh! Let's go on a trip."

"Okay. Where would you like to go?"

"Oh, I don't know." Thankfully, she dropped the subject.

But every few days she'd ask me the same questions. Sometimes she'd ask about a particular bank account and, after hearing the balance, she would say, "Do you need some money for anything?

Take some money and get yourself..." whatever struck her fancy that day. "My gift to you," she'd add.

She'd follow up a few days later by asking me to describe what I'd bought for myself with her money. I had to lie, because the only money I withdrew was to cover expenses on Mom's behalf. Lois, having experienced a similar situation with her mother, had stressed the importance of using Mom's own money to cover her expenses.

"As long as your mother has enough money for the things she needs or she wants, don't you dare buy it for her," Lois instructed. "You'll get to a point where you can't afford it, and then you will resent her and everything you have to do for her."

It was good advice. Although Mom's funds more than adequately covered her needs, the other Mom-related demands on my time and energy exhausted me, especially in the first six months. In time, Mom began to forget that she'd instructed me to make purchases for myself, and stopped asking me about them. It was a relief to stop making up stories.

Mom's confusion about her finances made it difficult to persuade her to relax her purse strings on her own behalf. In a fit of making-do during her second year at The Home, she covered the scuffs on the toes of her white sneakers with some kind of bright blue adhesive. Then she cut up her white silk pyjama top.

"For rags," she told Marg. After a long pause, she added, "Don't ask me why I needed rags."

I gave her new pyjamas for Christmas.

The word went around that the next family member to visit her would take her to buy new shoes—if she'd let one of us do that.

"If she doesn't want to pay for it, tell her it's a gift. Put it on your credit card and tell me how much it was so I can refund it," I said.

It didn't happen.

All her life, Mom had spent in unpredictable and impractical ways. She'd say yes to new skis, but she'd stick her old shoes or boots together with tape or glue. Yes to buying another ten table napkins and some Royal Minton china at the second-hand store, but no to replacing the leaking hot water heater. (She never used the good china, but she didn't seem to object to mopping water from the porch floor.) It was yes to treating everyone to a meal at a nice restaurant, where she invariably underestimated the cost, but no to spending an extra couple of dollars at the grocery store for a cut of beef she could actually chew. Yes to an expensive wool coat that didn't fit, (which she gave to me five years after she bought it) but no to replacing buttonless, ripped pyjamas, pilled and faded sweaters, or stretched and yellowed brassieres.

"So what? No one's going to see me," she'd say, adding with a little smirk, "More's the pity."

She'd always disguised her self-imposed penury well. She'd turn out to church smartly dressed, wearing lipstick and a snazzy scarf and beret. She'd place a hefty donation in the offering, and go home to eat overcooked leftovers heated in a burned-out pot and served on cracked dishes, while her pretty china sat gathering dust. Then she'd don old clothes fit only for rags and crawl into a jury-rigged bed made up with ripped quilts and sheets spread over a too-small mattress and a stack of shoeboxes.

The situation defied logic.

Or did it?

## CHAPTER 15

# If Wishes Were Horses

~❖~

*I* *wish I had asked Mom more questions about her life and demanded* more answers about her situation before all this happened—except I hadn't known before now what to ask.

For instance, except for preparing a will, a living will, and power of attorney documents, had Mom prepared herself emotionally or practically for the day when she would not be able to handle her own affairs?

She'd put off decisions and tasks until the days turned into weeks, months, and years. I deeply wish I'd prompted Mom to begin giving her possessions to the people she wanted to bequeath them to at least a decade earlier. I wish she'd thrown out all her useless and broken possessions long before I'd had to sort through her furniture, clothing, appliances, books, photos, and more. I wish I'd had my mother's help and involvement for all the downsizing and decision-making—while we were both a few years younger.

If—just if—Mom had started earlier to plan her move more precisely, deciding where she wanted to live and at what point she would be prepared to move, the transition would have been more gradual and easier on her and on everyone else.

If her house had already been sold or had been put on the market, there would have been less property tax to pay, fewer insurance fees, and fewer heating bills to pay while she was simultaneously making payments to The Home.

But while I wish the process had started earlier, there may never have been a perfect time to do what had to be done, and there's no point in wishing for what might have been.

"If wishes were horses, beggars would ride," the old saying goes.

~⋅~

*Even after years of researching and writing about seniors' issues as a* journalist, of listening to friends talk about their experiences with aging family members, of occasionally helping elderly friends with their moves, and of living in a community where most people are over the age of fifty-five, I had not been prepared for the amount of time and energy it had taken to settle Mom.

And I had not expected the experience to leave me wrung dry of energy, drive, and interest in life. My world became peculiarly flat and featureless for a while.

"The time and energy consumed on Mom's behalf is forever gone—selfish, but true," I wrote in my diary while wallowing in a swamp of self-pity. "My time was taken away from my husband, my children, my grandchildren, my friends, my work, my hobbies, my life, and I still have not found my feet. The experience chewed me up and spat me out, a quivering and exhausted glob on life's sidewalk." A poor-me moment—but real, and, thankfully, now past.

There is nothing new under the sun about aging parents needing care. Earlier generations cared for their elders within their homes and communities because almost everyone lived near one another, and care facilities for the elderly were few and far between. Choices were limited.

My European ancestors had sailed across the Atlantic a couple of hundred years ago or more, never to see their parents again. Like other men and women, they'd sallied forth for opportunity or adventure, to save the world as nurses or teachers or missionaries, to run away from difficult situations, or to follow a love interest. Once on this continent, they kept going, on the move to prove themselves, to find a better life, to fight for a cause. They left behind extended families who would grow old and need help, but the world was too big and disconnected for people to run back and forth between cities or across oceans, prairies, and mountains. Their parents got old and died, possibly without ever knowing whether their children had survived the ocean voyage, let alone whether they had settled well in the New World. Did the people who left their parents feel guilty? Did the siblings or cousins left behind to care for them feel resentment? Yes, I bet, to both.

When I was six, my father's father died. At the time, we lived on an island in northern Quebec, where getting in and out depended on weather, sporadic shipping schedules, and bush pilots who were either courageous or crazy.

A stroke several years earlier had meant Grandad had to be cared for at home by Gramma and Dad's sister. Dad managed to fly out every two years or so for conferences, and he would always take that opportunity to visit his family. In between, letters had to suffice. We had no phone, so we learned of Grandad's death by telegraph, too late for Dad to go to the funeral.

To me, my father's sadness was something I could reach out and feel with my hand. Gramma continued to live with my aunt, as chasing our family around Canada's hinterland was out of the question. Fifteen years later, Dad died suddenly, and then Gramma died about five years after him. To my surprise, my aunt expressed both joy at having her freedom from elder care, and anger at my late father that she had been the person to stay home with her aging parents all those years while he "went around having fun."

Until then I'd assumed, with the arrogance of comparative youth, that my aunt had chosen to stay with my grandparents.

"Your father got to go overseas and have all kinds of adventures," she fumed. "I stayed home and got a job and looked after Mom and Dad. I was responsible."

Dad had gone overseas to fight in a war, I told her—and he'd also had a job and was responsible for his family. But her sense of having been treated unjustly was firm. I remember wondering how many other people felt the same way: certainly not Marg's mother in looking after Gramps, or Marg, who cared for her mother. Neither spoke a word of complaint, but instead expressed a sense of loss at their passing, and a yearning for a new focus of care. Indeed, holding the reins for Mom's care has given me an odd sense of being honoured that I am finally able to do something for this stubbornly independent old woman.

Mom and I are fortunate to enjoy a loving and congenial relationship. And now that things are settled, we are no longer stressed, and I have learned some very important lessons. There are, and will always be, challenges. Being aware of them is part of my job. Awareness is not resentment, and it is not a reason to feel guilty. It has taken me some time to learn that.

~*~

*With Mom now settled, I expect to carry out her administrative tasks for the rest of her life, paying her bills and following up on her health care.* I did not expect it to take more than two years to sell the house, but I also didn't expect the benefits of Mom's move to The Home to be so quickly obvious.

The fees she pays to The Home are less than what it would have cost Mom to stay in her own house with the supports that would have allowed her to remain safe and healthy. Mom's food—three full meals a day and two snacks—laundry, and housecleaning are included in the flat rate for her residence fees. Services like haircuts, transportation to and from medical appointments, blood collection, and other incidentals are covered by a monthly comfort fund we deposit at The Home for her use. She has yet to spend the full monthly amount.

Mom has no bills for groceries, electricity, snow removal, property tax, home insurance, heating, or cleaning. She pays no maintenance costs, which were imminent at her house. In addition, she has ready access to a nurse, companionship with other residents, an in-house library, and on-site worship services. On cold days, she can exercise by walking around inside the building, and on fine days there are outdoor paths and benches.

She says she is happy; she speaks in glowing terms of the staff; she likes her room and her personal privacy: all she has to do is enter and close the door. She is in the right place, as settled as she will ever be.

Keeping Mom safe and happy is a team effort that involves Mom's doctor, The Home's staff, Marg and my other cousins, Auntie H., my brothers, Mom's grandchildren—and me. Keeping in touch with all those folks helps me know when she needs things like clothing, toiletries, mobility aids, distraction, or a trip to the doctor. Less obviously, our family's regular interaction with the staff and administrators of the facility make it clear that Mom has people who pay attention, and who are aware of what's going on in her life.

In early March 2020, before COVID-19 regulations clamped down on all activity, Howard and Lois visited Mom for her birthday, with a plan to enjoy a few days of skiing at a nearby resort. Fully masked and sanitized, they spent their first day with Mom. They took the time to Skype everyone to show them how well Mom looked.

Unfortunately, that very night, The Home was shut down when several residents, including Mom, suddenly developed diarrhea and vomiting. On the other side of the city, the ski hill shut down due to COVID-19 concerns. Lois and Howard swiftly changed their flights and flew back to Nova Scotia—just ahead of the order for all interprovincial travellers to self-isolate for two weeks.

The tummy illness at The Home proved to be temporary, but by the time everyone recovered, the doors had been closed against COVID-19. Mom and the other residents couldn't leave, and no one could visit. Marg went to Mom's window to wave hello, as did the Easter Bunny. My planned visit to Mom, which had included skiing for my husband, was put on indefinite hold. (As I write this, I have plans for a brief visit to Mom, wearing a mask and doused in sanitizer, before the pandemic goes into an expected second wave in the Atlantic provinces.)

At first Mom's memory loss meant she didn't notice the COVID restrictions—except to note that the staff who delivered meals to her room were now fully garbed in protective gear. After a few weeks, she asked me to visit. I had to tell her I couldn't. A few days later she complained that she was confined to quarters and wanted to move to Nova Scotia.

Not again! I explained that no one was allowed into, or out of, Nova Scotia. I also told her she was safer right where she was, at The Home: Nova Scotia's long-term care facilities were bearing the brunt of the pandemic in this province.

It was late May before residents were allowed outdoors to walk around the grounds, well-distanced from one another, and surrounded by signs warning outsiders to stay off the property. A photo taken from across the street and posted on Facebook showed Mom trundling her walker across The Home's parking lot, apparently on a mission. The image was more of a relief than I could have imagined.

I had expected the task of relocating Mom to The Home to be time-consuming, challenging, and demanding, with a steep learning curve. I hadn't expected a worldwide pandemic to keep us away from her after she'd moved. No one had.

There are, obviously, long-term care facilities with bad reputations, not enough staff, too many clients, inadequate procedures, and poor workplace ethics. In the wake of the COVID-19 pandemic and the numbers of deaths that have occurred in nursing homes, families like ours will likely become more vigilant and more inclined to speak up firmly if something concerns us—and also if something pleases us.

"You catch more flies with honey than with vinegar," Mom once told me.

Mom is lucky, in my opinion, to be in a place that is staffed by cheerful, dedicated, and competent people. She and I are at least a day's travel apart by the fastest route possible, and I have to put my trust in The Home. I believe it helps that they know I and my family members approve of them, that we all expect them to maintain their high standard of care, and that we want to work with them.

I hope they never let me—or Mom—down. So far, The Home's precautions against COVID-19 seem to be working: no cases have been reported there. Knock wood!

Perhaps ironically, the lockdown during the COVID-19 pandemic gave me the time and space to actually relax, recover, and begin to find myself again. It was an unexpected upside to a worldwide disaster for which few were prepared. I have finally had time to reflect—a luxury I couldn't earlier afford. In fact, I have been making up for lost time, aided by the COVID-19 shutdown that liberates me from community demands.

Mom told me that staying in her room can get dreary, but it's not too bad.

"Where would I go, anyway? The weather has been awful," she says. "We take turns going to the dining room and we have to stay sixteen [according to her] feet apart. The rest of the time they bring me my meals on a tray. The girls are all covered up. My God, they are wonderful, you know!"

The Home is relatively small, more like an actual home than a "facility," which may make it easier to practice infection control measures, but most of the COVID-19 pandemic seems to have flown under Mom's radar.

"You should drop in to see me," she said, about sixty days into the lockdown.

"Mom, I'm not even allowed out of Nova Scotia."

"Oh, that's right. Well, some day soon."

Indeed!

~⚬~

*I can't underestimate the value of the support we had from the entire* extended family during the process of moving Mom into The Home. It was a happy circumstance that my brothers and I and our families had been able to cooperate to support Mom's resettlement. It would have been a more difficult task if we hadn't been able to consult with one another or if we'd argued over every decision. We held together, and we became closer—an item for the plus side of the family ledger.

Looking back, Mom's complete withdrawal from the battle-field—so to speak—had also been helpful. It had allowed us to make decisions without being second-guessed. Despite her lack of preparation, she'd agreed to the move and had actually encouraged the sale of the house. She could have held on to the doorjambs for dear life and been dragged out kicking and biting. Well, not bit-ing—she hasn't enough teeth! But she could have been angry and refused to speak to us for years. It happens, but it didn't with Mom.

In the end, it's important to say that she—and we, her family—are fortunate in so many ways. My mother can still get out of her bed, walk around, wash, feed, and dress herself, take herself to the toilet, read the paper, and talk on the phone. (She may refuse to do any number of these things, but she is capable.)

I have to admit, though, that I currently have no plan for the time when she can no longer carry out those tasks. If or when it happens, I can only hope for a gentle transition to the next stage of her care.

CHAPTER 16

# Lessons Learned

~❧~

*T*he past couple of years have been an education. When I started this journey with Mom, I had no idea what I didn't know.

My life experience to that point had led me to believe that if I was dogged enough in my search for information and in my efforts to achieve something on Mom's behalf, it would happen. I had no idea how much patience would be required—and how much would continue to be required, even after I thought everything had been sorted out.

For instance, more than a year after Mom moved into The Home, and several months past her 91st birthday, her change-of-address notifications had still not all taken effect. I thought that, by then, everyone from the Prime Minister to the paper boy knew where she'd moved. But no. In the middle of the next year's tax season, a batch of T-slips was sent to her former address by the Canada Revenue Agency. Fortunately her mail was still being forwarded to me by the post office.

That should not have happened. Copies of Mom's power of attorney document and a change of address notification had been sent to every corner of officialdom that had ever sent anything to her. Trying to fix the situation became a three-ring circus with dancing elephants.

First, I called the Canada Pension Plan office, where those particular slips had originated, but the administrators were hidden deep behind a wall that would have held back Genghis Khan. There was no "press a number" option for changing an address, so I pressed all the buttons in turn in an effort to reach a real live person. I found one, but it immediately went dead—the line, not the person. I hope.

I called my Member of Parliament, where an assistant put me on hold while she went to find out how I could change the address.

"Call the Canada Revenue Agency," she said when she came back.

"The number in the front of the phone book?"

"Yes."

She was in a hurry. Busy times in parliament, apparently.

I called the number in the book, only to hear a robot tell me to go online and create an account as all their telephone-answering people were too busy to answer the phone. "How many 91-year-old pensioners have access to the internet? Or know how to create a damned account?" I muttered as I hung up and went to the CRA website.

The site asked for Mom's Social Insurance Number—no problem. Her postal code? I typed in the one on the wrongly-addressed T-slips, on the principle that it was the address they had in their records.

Wrong.

I typed in my postal code. Correct, but odd. If they had a record of Mom's new address as my place, why didn't they use it?

Next question: How much did she pay in taxes, per line 120 of her last return?

It took me five minutes to dig out the return and find line 120. I checked twice that I had the correct number and typed it in.

Then I had to create a user name and password, and was told a login ID would be mailed to me. I asked to have it emailed to me instead, and filled in my email address.

The user name is too similar to the password, the robot told me. Do it again, using something easy to remember that no one else would guess.

Okay.

You need to set up security questions and answers, it told me. I had five choices from five lists of questions, and I had to provide five case-specific answers. I wrote them in a notebook. It took a good fifteen minutes of reading the options to figure out which questions would have the easiest answers for me, or for Howard as Mom's standby power of attorney. After I'd completed the whole the form, I received a message saying that the security questions would be unnecessary in future if I logged on from "this device."

I clicked submit.

Session timed out, it said.

Gritting my teeth, I started over, typing in exactly the same information as I had the first time. Wrong, it said.

How could it be? Then I realized that this time it had asked for a different line from the previous year's tax return. I scrambled through the papers and found the number before I got timed out again. I filled in all the blanks again, and tapped submit.

Internal error, it told me. Try again later. I could feel a black cloud forming over my head. I called the Canada Revenue Agency and sat on hold for thirty-five minutes. Finally, a pleasant voice answered, only to tell me that I'd called the wrong place.

"Call Service Canada," she said. I drew a deep breath and exhaled slowly as I hung up the phone. This was all I could do that day; a looming appointment meant Service Canada would have to wait until the next day.

Service Canada was not in the phone book. Instead, the government pages listed individual services covered by Service Canada, under a multitude of acronyms: EI, CPP, OAS, CRA, HST, GST. Since I'd already had no luck with the number for CPP, I went online again to find a number to call. I dialled, swearing under my breath about the expectation that elderly people could easily complete this kind of wild goose chase.

I stopped muttering when The Voice said my call was being recorded. No doubt they've heard a lot of choice comments in those recordings. The Voice correctly predicted a five- minute wait.

When a human answered, I explained the situation again, as calmly and as clearly as possible. The woman wanted Mom to come to the phone to verify that I had permission to change her address.

"Well, no, she's in Newfoundland."

"Oh, you told me that. I'm sorry. Can she call me herself?"

At that point, after almost a year at The Home, Mom had called me fewer than a dozen times, and each time seemed surprised that she'd reached me. Soon after her move, when the phone company wanted her approval on some matter, my cousin Marg had volunteered to help her make the call. Mom had been confused, and then angry that she was confused. After that, she would just wave her hand and say, "Monica will look after it!"

How do you explain all that to a stranger at a call centre?

"No, she has trouble even calling me," I said.

"Do you have power of attorney?"

I'd mentioned that in my first sentence, but I suppose it is hard to remember everything a stranger tells you over the phone.

"Yes."

"You'll have to send a certified copy to us."

"Can I email it?"

Mom's employment pension service had allowed me to scan and email the document to them. "No, I'm sorry, but you can take the original to the nearest Service Canada office. They will make a certified copy for us and return the original to you."

After explaining that Mom's lawyer had the original and all I had were copies, I was told to mail it and ask for it back. In the same letter, I could ask to have the address changed.

---

### Service Canada

Service Canada is designed to act as a single access point for Canada's most-used federal programs. It is operated by Employment and Social Development Canada and has offices across the country. What does Service Canada handle? A lot, it turns out.

- Social Insurance numbers
- Employment Insurance
- Passport services
- Old Age Security
- Canada Pension Plan
- Retirement planning
- Caregiving benefits
- Survivor allowances
- Benefits-finding
- Fraud awareness
- The GST/HST credit
- A job bank

(Source: Canada.ca.)

"Be sure to put both the old and new addresses," she said. A few pleasantries, and we hung up.

Argh! I'd forgotten to ask where to send the document. I went back online to find a mailing address. Too many choices! Should I mail it to St. John's or to Halifax? I opted to mail it to St. John's, to the office that had generated the tax slips.

~*~

*Service Canada still hadn't responded to my letter by the time the next* federal election rolled around, and Mom's voting card, generated from income tax data, landed in my mailbox. She was supposed to vote at the polling station near me.

I wanted to scream.

I'd worked a few times for Elections Canada and knew how the system was supposed to work. However, the reason they had employed me and so many others at election time was to try to fix the plethora of mistakes in addresses and assigned polling stations. I say "try" because few of the interventions seemed to work. Voters were still steered to the wrong polls on election day. I could imagine Mom's wrath if she tried to vote and was told she wasn't on the list.

I remembered that residents of special-care homes were supposed to be enumerated before elections, so there was a good chance that Mom was on the rolls. I called The Home.

"Don't worry," the administrator said. "Everyone in here is from somewhere else. We're used to this. We have to look after getting voters registered for every election."

I hoped that wouldn't lead the Canada Revenue Agency to revert to mailing her tax information to The Home. Meanwhile, the St. John's tax office still hadn't returned that power of attorney document. Reminding them was another item on my to-do list.

⁓⁂⁓

*If you are going through this kind of experience, or something similar, know* this: it is natural and normal to feel tired, preoccupied, and over-taxed, although better words to describe my state early in the process of settling Mom would have been exhausted, disoriented, and—occasionally—a feeling of being hunted by the hounds of hell. Awareness and recognition of our feelings can keep us from taking our anxieties and frustrations out on our spouses, children, and friends, and can prompt us to take care of our own health and well-being.

The first rule of first aid is to prevent further injury, including injury to ourselves as the rescuers. The first rule of medicine is to do no harm, including harm to ourselves as the caregivers. We can't help someone else if we are broken and helpless.

I've also learned that it's important not to blame the person in our care for our exhaustion and confusion. It is important to always remember—and even to repeat several times a day, when things go squirrelly—"It is not her fault that she needs me. She doesn't want to need me. She can't help it." At the end of every recitation it also doesn't hurt to ask, "How would I want to be treated if I was in her place?"

As I've discovered, these things are easy to know on an intel-lectual level but harder to remember when a parent behaves like an obnoxious toddler. At that point we may be tempted to react without thinking. In those moments, my advice is to just breathe. Count backwards from a million. Walk away if it's safe to do so. It can be particularly hard to exercise that kind of patience if we don't realize that our parent suffers from an invisible challenge like memory loss, hearing loss, vision loss, or the inability to properly comprehend or navigate the world around them.

Another thing I've learned is that looking after an adult, especially a parent, is absolutely not the same as caring for a child. New parents have the benefit of preparation, buckets of advice, and the joy that surrounds a new life. Our parents already have well-defined personalities, and often have a habit of not listening to what their youngsters advise them to do. To them, we are just kids—what do we know about anything?

When we become their caregivers, though, they are still our parents. As far back as we can remember, they've looked after themselves, and they've looked after us, too. How can it be that, suddenly, they simply can't do it any longer? Logically, we get it. But when you have spent fifty years or more respecting your parents for their wisdom and ability, and that all flies out the window, it's an emotional blow, even when you can see it coming.

~*~

*There is no education as effective as hands-on learning, but advice from* other people with similar experiences is almost as good.

It turns out I am not the only person swamped in ignorance about looking after an aging parent and his or her property and legacy. Many of my friends and relatives are in the same situation as myself —the curse of the baby boomers—and sometimes we connect to commiserate and share stories. Individually, every person in that situation might feel overwhelmed, but together, our collective knowledge is encyclopedic. We all want to vent, and there is plenty to complain about.

One friend's elder demanded daily visits from family members; they refused to eat, socialize, or do much else until that visit took place. No amount of explanation or cajoling helped, and the guilt wore out the family—especially the person who visited most and needed a break. The lesson I took away from that family's experience? I'd done the right thing by not visiting or calling Mom every day after she'd moved.

If families can agree on a plan for their parents' care, the outcome will be better for everyone. If they can't, in some jurisdictions a government agency may assume responsibility for the person's care, and for the elder's income and assets. That situation, of course, comes with its own problems.

It also helps to figure out in advance where all the "stuff" is going to go. Horror stories about families infighting over their parents' dishes, paintings, or other belongings can be avoided if designated recipients for all those items are identified years ahead of time. Even then, it may not work out. A friend's mother wanted to turn forty years of *Chatelaine* magazines over to a local school, but her plan fell through when the school refused the donation.

"Just do what you can do with the stuff and don't tell your mother," was the lesson she offered from that experience. "If she asks, tell her it has a good home, even if the home is the furnace. Then change the subject. Only lie if you have to!"

An elderly acquaintance of mine had been a sweet old gentleman until he'd developed dementia, at which point he'd become physically violent and verbally abusive to his wife. He was ultimately placed in a secure unit in a nursing home, where his loyal wife visited him daily until his death. "Remember, that's not the real person," she told me. "Just ignore it, and when they get ornery, walk away until next time."

Her advice came to mind whenever Mom took out her anger on various people. I shouldn't hold it against her: it was not the "real Mom."

In the early days of memory loss, family members may believe the forgetful person hasn't been listening or wasn't paying attention to something they'd just been told. "Don't bother arguing with anyone who has dementia—even mild dementia," I was advised many times, by people who had experienced it with their own parents. "Don't even tell them when they repeat themselves. It never works, and it's not worth the trouble. Just go along with them, even if all you say is, 'Hmmmm.' Then change the subject the first chance you get."

That valuable piece of advice—when I remembered to put it to use—helped me avoid many confrontations. Now it surprises me to hear someone remind a forgetful person, "You just told me that." It's not just a waste of time; it can lead to angry conflict.

Other valuable advice I received: keep everyone in the family informed of Mom's changing circumstances. You might need someone else to step in to help if you get sick. I've tried to follow that advice, though it's easier with people who are interested than with those who never ask questions. Regardless, they can't say they haven't been kept in the loop.

"Don't spend your own money on their needs while they have money, and keep track of every cent," Lois had advised. That simple advice was easy for me to follow: my financial situation simply did not allow me to spend my own money on Mom's care and housing. Mom's pensions and savings are enough to cover her expenses, of which she appears to have few. She is past the stage of shopping for pleasure, as it exhausts her, and she has almost everything she needs. I record any payments I make on Mom's behalf, keep copies of bills and cheques and online payment statements, and maintain a file of digital accounts. The documents might sit in my file tray for weeks, but I do keep them—not just as proof of transactions, but also as aide-memoires. My "Mom file" also helps me keep track of tasks I've done on her behalf—everything from contacting her doctor to preparing her tax returns.

Mom never did remember her lawyer's name. It was a lucky break that I found Ms. M.'s bill among the papers at the house or I might still be searching. The lesson: share that kind of information with your family. They will need to know.

The sale and distribution of my mother's house and its contents were left to Howard's and my discretion. The best advice, from those who'd been through it, varied from "don't throw out

## Don't Throw It Out!

- Tax receipts, T-slips, tax returns (for at least seven years)
- Bank, investment, credit, loan, and other financial documents
- Medical reports, receipts, or records
- Provincial health cards
- Insurance information
- Certificates, licenses, registrations
- Identification cards
- Bills
- Sales receipts for big-ticket items

- Warranties
- Contracts
- Deeds and survey reports
- Addresses and phone numbers
- Recent personal letters or cards
- Calendars, appointment books, diaries
- Notes scrawled on envelopes, in notebooks, or on bits of paper (until you are absolutely sure they are no longer needed)
- And don't forget to check between the pages of books and magazines!

any papers" to "keep only the important papers." I took a middle path, but Mom's off-and-on filing system was certainly a puzzle.

~✻~

*Despite my experience in researching seniors' issues when I was a reporter,* it turns out I didn't fully understand the continuing care system in my own province, much less the one in Newfoundland and Labrador or elsewhere. With Mom, I had to start from the beginning.

To complicate the situation, procedures and responsibilities vary among provinces, between municipalities, and across time. For example, seniors' low-income housing programs, once handled by the Nova Scotia Department of Community Services, now fall under the umbrella of Housing Nova Scotia, a provincial government agency that works with regional Housing Authorities across the province. Long-term care facilities come under the Department of Health and Wellness. Just across the Northumberland Strait in Prince Edward Island, Health PEI handles long-term care, while the Department of Social Development oversees long-term care in New Brunswick. Often, the various websites haven't caught up with the legislation, and even employees whose job it is to advise callers may be uninformed about resources they may deal with infrequently.

Anyone trying to collect information about long-term care would be well advised to get any promises in writing, and to have a trusted person with them as a second set of eyes and ears when consulting the various agencies.

The Nova Scotia Department of Seniors coordinates information about all provincial programs that might apply to seniors. It has information about health, housing, adult education, safety, abuse, finances, and more. The department can be accessed at novascotia.ca/seniors, with a toll-free number listed in the government pages of the phone book. That website has a link to The Positive Aging Directory, a guide to many programs and services for seniors in Nova Scotia. You can read the directory online, download a PDF, or request a print version via the website—meaning that essentially the only way to get the publication is to go online, a situation that annoys me. Not every senior has internet access or wants to learn the intricacies of searching the web. As a test, I phoned to ask for a print copy and got a recording asking me to leave a message and a call-back number. I hung up, my excuse being that I am officially a senior with no patience for phone messages.

I found similar seniors' services directories available in most provinces across Canada, either in print or as digital files. My advice is to request a print copy and keep it with your telephone book. Fold a small piece of tape as a tab on the edges of the most-used pages. It will save you the time you would have spent traipsing all over the internet when you need help immediately.

Every province and territory in Canada offers a 211 information service. Dialing 211 puts you in touch with a real person who can direct you to the health and social services resources you might need from community groups, non-profits, or government departments. Each regional location also has a website. When I called and explained that I was researching for a book, a knowledgeable, enthusiastic responder didn't pass me off to a public relations person, but took ample time to explain how 211 works. A typical day at work for her could mean connecting seniors to housing authorities, medical care, legal assistance, people who can help them fill out applications, or almost anything or anyone—around the clock.

## Telephone Tips

- If you are angry, calm down before making a call. An angry question usually gets a defensive response. You want their help, not their excuses.
- Before calling, write down what you want to know.
- Turn off the television or mute other distractions before dialling.
- Avoid speakerphone if possible, because it may distort reception, and because you may be discussing sensitive private subjects.
- State your name and your reason for calling ("I want information about...").
- If you don't understand the answers, or you have more questions—ask.
- There is no such thing as a stupid question.
- If you're dissatisfied with the response, ask if there is someone else who can help.
- Even if you think you know the answers, get official confirmation.
- Be unfailingly polite and calm, but firm.
- Take your time.
- Write down the information you receive—carefully!
- Final question: "Is there anything else I should have asked?"

In Newfoundland and Labrador, the St. John's-based SeniorsNL, a voluntary organization operated by a board of directors, offers links to numerous provincial and national resources and provides an online guide called Seniors Guide to Services and Programs in NL. The province's Department of Health and Community Services also has a section devoted to seniors.

Most of my experiences in dealing with the agencies I contacted on Mom's behalf were positive, but sometimes you don't know what questions to ask or how to ask them—understandable when you're thrown into the deep end of senior care. Regardless, if you want to know something, ask—and keep asking until you understand the answer. The worst that can happen is that you'll be refused or referred to someone else.

## CHAPTER 17

# Where the Apple Falls

❦

*M*oving Mom was complicated and shocking and a wakeup call about my own situation.

I am not planning on going anywhere soon, but no one here is getting any younger. The day will come for me to move on—to a more manageable living space, to a continuing care home, or to... whatever comes after I shuffle off this mortal coil.

I know now that my stuff can't come with me, and it's mortifying to imagine my children sorting through my belongings. I can hear them now:

"Why did Mom keep a drawer full of pencil stubs and rotten elastic bands?"

"Why did she have seven bottles of glue, all open?"

"What's with the mountains of yogurt containers [black leotards/wine corks/broken shells/holey socks/coat hangers]?"

"Oh, my! The paper!"

I know that without intervention now, my mess will only get worse. I will forget, not only where I've put things, but that I own them at all. My physical health will undoubtedly deteriorate with age, preventing me from tidying and cleaning anything but my nearest possessions. The closet depths, the high shelves, the crawl spaces, and the heavy items will be ignored. I will be just like Mom.

The apple doesn't fall far from the tree.

But I don't want to go there. I don't want to tread in Mom's footsteps when it comes to clutter, late-in-life decisions, and the disposition of my assets. I want to be prepared, unburdened.

But how should I begin? Even wondering about that first over-whelming step gave me insight into Mom's behaviour. She didn't know where to start, but I've decided to find out by seeking advice about moving, legal issues, and downsizing.

Reading about something is easier than doing it (or even writing about it), so I hit the books first—and as part of my newly turned leaf I borrowed them from the community library instead of buying them.

These books offered tips ranging from the silly to the sensible. For example, in *The Life-Changing Magic of Tidying Up*, Japanese cleaning guru Marie Kondo suggests I hold each possession in my hands. If it gives me joy, I should keep it. If it does not, she advises me to thank the item for its service and say goodbye to it. Then find it a new home: send it to the dump, burn it, do whatever it takes.

I had to laugh. Sorry, Ms. Kondo, it would take me more years than I have left to hold each of my possessions and converse with them. Besides, so many things give me joy I can't imagine doing without them—like the ridiculous china figurine of a chubby sun-bather bulging from her swimsuit that was a gift from my sister-in-law (and which makes me laugh every time I look at it), and photos of my faraway grandkids that smile blessings at me whenever I glance from my daily tasks. On the other hand, my bucket and string mop give me no joy, but I do like them more than crawling around the floor with a wet rag.

On Kondo's advice, though, I did get rid of the ugly flowerpot that held all my scissors, including some child-safe pairs that I no longer needed—no more children here! I moved the sharp scissors to a desk drawer—after chucking out a broken stapler, cartridges for a non-existent fountain pen, and some other detritus. Useful items went into a giveaway box with the kids' scissors and the flowerpot, and before I knew it I had freed up a square foot of desk space.

Kondo's most valuable insight is that tidying up is not simply about storing all of one's possessions. That subtlety had previously escaped Mom and me. Like most people, we equate tidying up with finding a place for everything and putting everything in its place. Kondo's advice about eliminating items which have no practical use or that give us no joy would have led us to clear out two-thirds of Mom's junk—and mine, which might not have been a bad thing.

Mom's century-old house had no basement and no attic for storage, and her Depression-era upbringing wouldn't allow her to discard anything that might someday be of use, so the only solution for her had been to create storage places in the form of shelves, hooks, rods, wheelie bins, trunks, totes, and boxes. She hid her stuff behind doors, in closets, behind appliances, under beds, and under tables. She filled two outbuildings, the porch, the hallway, the washroom, the cavity under the stairs, and the high cupboards.

"Things to put things in" were among Mom's favourite purchases.

She had saved everything. So many years after Dad's death, it was hard to fathom that Mom still had all his letters—unsorted, still creased and folded in their original envelopes, untouched over the past forty-six years.

Unlike me, Mom had an excuse. Immediately after Dad died, she'd had to throw everything into boxes and move. The boxes followed her everywhere she moved, until she finally retired to her father's house. She had put off dealing with the boxes' contents for so long, she barely remembered she had them.

In another of my library finds, *The Gentle Art of Swedish Death Cleaning*, author Margareta Magnusson advises us to share our treasures long before we get old and die. Few people can accurately predict the date of their demise, but as we get older, we know it's getting closer. Giving our precious items away while we are still alive instead of leaving them in a will allows us to observe the recipients' joy and gratitude, Magnussen says. As well, we gain the satisfaction of decluttering our personal spaces for whatever time we have left.

---

### *How to Know When You've Got Clutter*

- You use only mugs, but you own dozens of cups and saucers.
- You have CDs, tapes, and records that you haven't played in years.
- Your stash of wedding announcements and greeting cards smells mouldy (and you don't remember the people who sent some of them).
- You have expired medications in the bathroom cabinet.
- You haven't worn some of your costume jewellery since the 70s.
- Your pile of "things to be fixed" is at least five years old.
- You own shoes with cracked soles, no laces, and busted toes.
- Your children are parents and you still have their baby clothes.
- You don't know what is in the back of the closet—any closet.

Taking Magnusson's advice, I was delighted to give away my handmade chess set that had languished in a drawer, unused, for years. A few weeks later my youngest grandchildren, who would actually use and enjoy them, received our toboggan and handmade sled. My set of crystal stemware that is currently gathering dust in its custom-made racks will be next. (I'd earned the glasses by collecting juice labels thirty years ago—proof, actually, that saving garbage can be rewarding.)

Here is a bit of personal advice from me: if your senior relative wants to give you something, help them by taking whatever they offer: the ugly lamp, the old photo albums, the cracked china, the useless bedding, the ancient bicycle seat. You can throw it in a garbage bin or deliver it to a charity thrift shop on the way home. You can take it home and laugh at it, examine it for hidden money or valuable share certificates before you throw it out, or pass it on to someone else. You can keep it because you like it, or to remind you that someday you may end up just like your parents—with too much stuff and nowhere to put it. Whatever, just take it. You will be doing the old folks a favour.

When my children began leaving home twenty-five years ago, I attacked some of my clutter by following the command of home-organizing wizard Marla Cilley, aka Fly Lady, to throw out one thing a day. Unfortunately, that thing was often something already destined for the garbage and it was also often replaced with two new things—so not really a success for me, as strategies go.

A few years later I experimented with the "Clutter Busting" method developed by Brooks Palmer, which aimed to rid one's life of physical and emotional clutter. He advised setting a timer and vigorously sorting and clearing one spot until the time was

up. The practice allowed me to tidy drawers and corners, but did
not reduce the overall mass, which was simply stored more neatly
in new places.

I gave up. Life is too short, I said.

—⚹—

*With all my reading out of the way, I decided it was finally time to take*
action. Deducing that I could eliminate much of my stash by using
it up, I began to finish abandoned craft projects. It didn't take me
long to remember why they'd been abandoned: they consumed
valuable time. I complained about the work involved—just as Mom
had wished out loud for family to visit to help her sort—until it
got on my family's nerves.

"Jeez, Mom, stop worrying about it," my youngest said to me
when I moaned about trying to clean out my junk. "If it's a lot of
trouble, we'll handle it when the time comes. You and Dad enjoy
yourselves, and enjoy all your stuff."

He's a good son, but I could enjoy my stuff more if I could
find it.

His comments prompted me to change tactics. I decided I
would carry out the sorting, organizing, using up and/or chucking
out of clutter as a stealth campaign: a bit at a time, addressing the
hidden clutter first.

At Christmas, when I took things out of storage to decorate,
I actually discarded the broken decorations. I took digital photos
of the decorations I planned to sell or give away the following
November—and stored the decorations in a separate box until then.
I continued to take photos of other items to sell online.

During the long winter evenings after the holidays I turned hundreds of scenic photos into greeting cards, while my husband watched his favourite television shows. This was win/win/win: I got to spend time with my husband, I used up materials that had been left over from my scrapbooking craze, I created a stash of greeting cards (which I never remember to buy until it's too late), I emptied a box of photos, and I cleared out some office space.

That success encouraged me to continue to find ways to use up my stuff. For years, I had ruled that for every new thing that came in, one old thing must go. Old clothing went as far as the rag bag, leading to an overabundance of rags—which I now make an effort to use instead of paper towels. For years, I'd collected candle stubs in an old stew pot; the plan was to melt them down during the winter when the wood stove was going and make them into new candles. Finally, I bought wicks, got out the stew pot, and made candles—a lot of candles. There's just one problem: after all that effort, the wax is still here cluttering up my house. It's been changed into candles, but it's still taking up space. Let's put that in the "never again" category.

More recently, I delivered two big bags of textiles (discarded clothing and unwanted sewing fabric) to a local business that turns it all into new useful items. Call me happy! Other hobby supplies are still jammed into cupboards and boxes in our house and outbuildings. Some—like sewing, gardening, and preserving supplies—date from the time when we couldn't afford to buy things so we learned to make them. We no longer need to make them, but we still have the equipment. We have stuff related to photography and silviculture, outdoor sports, music, and paint-ing. I made up a six-page list to help me decide what to do with it all—but I'm damned if I can remember where I put the list! We also have leftovers from building and maintaining our house for more than forty-five years. We haven't gotten rid of so much as a 1970s ceiling tile in case we need it someday—presuming we can find it when that day arrives.

One of the obstacles to looking after our clutter is that we sometimes hesitate to ask for help. Looking back, I realize that Mom had asked for help several times, framed as, "I wish someone would come to visit so they could help me clean out my closet...," or whatever space she had in mind. But few people want to take their annual vacations to go and clean someone's closet or shed.

Nor do most visitors, even close family members, feel comfortable just taking things. If Mom had once said, "My dear, I'd like you to have this," I might have clued in to her motives. But it would have been really helpful if she had told me who was to receive what. At one point, I'd helped her start a list of all the family members and what she wanted them to have, but I found it, untouched and unfinished, months after she'd moved out. The only things she'd designated from her overflowing house were my grandmother's table and sideboard. (She'd once told my daughter "write your name on something if you want it." My daughter had, but then Mom offered the item to someone else. It all ended well, but it made us wary.)

We could all probably benefit from the help of the kinds of professional organizers who make a career out of helping people downsize. They call it "rightsizing," recognizing that people's needs change over time and that our possessions should reflect that progression. Professional organizers, sometimes also called move managers, don't force their clients to make decisions or to discard all their treasures. Instead, they patiently walk them through the sorting, designating, organizing, moving, and resettling process.

The cost of their help can range from hundreds to tens of thousands of dollars. That sort of expense may scare some seniors, but it's likely worth every penny for someone who does not have family or friends who are able or willing to help. As a dedicated do-it-yourselfer, I don't need, and can't afford, that kind of help. But those services are beginning to look better with every passing year. (See Appendix C: Move Managers and Professional Organizers on page 227.)

～＊～

*Theoretically, given that we're younger, my husband and I have more* time than Mom had to change our ways. That's good, because we have twice the stuff she had, and we rarely agree on what to keep and what to toss. He thinks most of my possessions are ripe for elimination, but wants to keep all of his stuff. I think exactly the opposite, of course.

My office is an example. As my writing refuge, it's my best argument for never moving from this house. It's painted in my favourite colours, with ergonomically correct furniture and all the necessary word- and photo-processing equipment. My husband built the ample bookshelves holding my collection of research materials and inspirational books from maple that was grown, cut, and sawn on our property. My office is where I pay bills, conduct business, file documents, practise music, and do so much more. It's a busy room.

My husband and I shared this space until he received a tablet one Christmas. Now the living room is his office; the coffee table is covered in Very Important Scribbled Notes and its tiny drawer is so full it barely opens. It gives me no joy at all, but no matter what Marie Kondo says, I won't touch it. Neither have I touched his twenty-year-old computer, still on a desk next to mine, disconnected and unused. The decision to get rid of it will have to be made by both of us. So far, it's pending.

Then there's the issue of how to dispose of our joint financial assets. _The Canadian Guide to Will and Estate Planning_ has good advice, but I should have read it in my 40s. It's too late now to hide my wealth in funny places to protect my kids from taxes. However, I would recommend the book to anyone who owns any property at all, and who understands that two plus two can sometimes equal five—if the two and two are handled correctly.

On the positive side, my husband and I have actually made wills. We made the first one years ago before we went on a vacation and left the children with friends. We bought a form and filled it out, naming executors and getting our signatures witnessed—the whole schtick. A few years later, after all the youngsters had left home and life had changed, we planned another trip. We owned a computer by that time, so we bought will-preparation software and followed the instructions. A friend with probate experience looked at it and pronounced it as good as any she'd seen, included those prepared by lawyers.

"You just saved the price of your trip," she said.

Since then, things have changed again: we have more grandchildren, property, junk, and papers. We are also quite a bit older, so contemplating making a new will is more tiring, and also more urgent, than what we've done leading up to now.

I don't know if it will be possible for us to get away with a computer-generated will any longer. A writers' organization recently informed me that I own intellectual property that must be designated in a will. My books, unpublished manuscripts, and all my writing—even love letters and grocery lists—may be valuable someday (fingers crossed). As their creator, I hold the copyright, but I'd never considered it to be worth mentioning in a will. My husband, a sometimes-artist, also needs to worry about intellectual property. His few sculptures, and the plans and drawings for them, may be worth more than all my books put together, even though he refuses to sell them during his lifetime. Neither of us has had time to think about our intellectual property, so it's become a stressor, another set of tasks on the to-do list—shoved to the backs of our minds until it becomes urgent.

I swear, people must die just to get away from these chores.

~⁕~

*Then there's the matter of our final wishes. An illness last year had me* crawling up the stairs on my hands and knees—making it clear that the time had finally come to seriously consider my own arrangements.

A couple of funeral homes, in an effort to get my business, had sent out pamphlets with advice on how to count my assets, make out my will, and prepare my funeral. As if I would be there to enjoy it! What part of "I'm dead, people! I don't care!" do they not understand? But I'm told one has to consider the people left behind, and that these things should be looked after to make it easier for them. Maybe. I haven't decided what I'll do, but I know I hate funerals.

Mom has decided what she wants, though.

"I want to be cremated," she announced one day recently. "Take a few of my ashes and poke them in on top of your father. Do you think you could do that?"

Dad had been buried outside a church that was deconsecrated thirty-five years after his death and then sold as a storage facility, leaving a handful of graves on the front yard surrounded by an iron fence.

"I think I could," I replied, my mind busy with the implications of "poking" Mom "on top" of my father, and how I might disguise a cup of ashes as potting soil when I climbed over the fence to "plant crocuses" on Dad's final resting place.

"I don't care what you do with the rest of me," Mom added.

I don't know what to do with the rest of her, either, although the possibilities abound. It's not like we're going to forget Mom, wherever her last resting place may be. She is—as you've clearly seen by now—unforgettable.

⁓⁎⁓

*My husband and I are both now on the sunset side of sixty, with too-short futures ahead, piles of stuff to deal with, and to-do lists that are way too long!* When we enter our own versions of The Home, or when we die, we want our children to know our wishes.

It sounds harsh, but it's realistic: I need to have a life plan that will work if I am alone. Single. Right now, my husband and I are both able-bodied, but if and when one of us becomes seriously incapacitated or dies, the other of us will be left alone to deal with what is, essentially, a two-person set of difficult tasks. If that's going to be me, I want to know my options. If I was alone in this remote home, emptied of half the humans and half the stuff that occupies the space, would I rattle around like a pea in a drum—lonely, isolated and overwhelmed?

Having to look after the housekeeping, cutting and hauling firewood, snow removal, lawn and garden care, car care, bill-paying and other administrative tasks, indoor and outdoor home maintenance and repair, shopping, and cooking would all be daunting for a person living alone. I admire Mom for carrying on as long as she did!

Several years before Mom's move, I'd found a list aimed at helping seniors decide on their future living arrangements. It was old-fashioned computer accordion-fold printout, the kind with holes down the edges and perforations for tearing apart the pages.

According to the list, the first possibility upon finding oneself alone in the family home is to just carry on. Do the necessary jobs and ignore everything else until it slides into a crisis of disrepair and danger when, hopefully, a family member or friend will come to the rescue and take care of things. Clearly this is not the best option. For me, that would mean either learning to do the daily jobs my husband currently does, hiring someone to do them, or letting them go undone. Of course, he would have the same choices if he were the one left alone.

This had been Mom's route, but I don't believe she'd intended to take it, or even realized it was happening at the time. She probably thought she still had lots of time to make decisions.

The list's second option is to reduce the number of tasks by immediately eliminating responsibilities. That would require the dreaded sorting and selling of possessions—including the house, which would, in turn, mean making a quick—and possibly the wrong—decision about where to live next.

The third option is to suck it up and start immediately to reduce our overall number of tasks and responsibilities. That would allow us to age in place in this house—to live here for longer with less work. It also involves sorting, designating, and eliminating possessions, and it means making repairs that will outlast the survivor.

A better option: we should decide now what kind of lifestyle we'd like to have in ten or twenty years—should we live that long—and what we can actually manage. I use the pronouns "we" and "us" because this is my preferred plan!

Over the past ten years, a number of our neighbours have died or moved, and their houses have changed hands. We don't know the new residents very well: they are younger and busier with their children and their jobs. As a result, we've intermittently discussed rightsizing or selling some land to fund our old age. We've also toyed with selling everything to buy a smaller house, or moving to a condo or apartment. We've made lists of what we can't do without, discovering that we want plenty of outdoor space, natural surroundings, an office for me, a workshop studio for him, and privacy—somewhere in this same area. We've even looked around, but nothing was as good as the house we have. Obviously, we are not ready to leave yet.

Staying will require adding age-friendly amenities like grab bars, ramps, wider doorways, a more efficient heating system to reduce our dependence on labour-intensive firewood, and a second bathroom to allow us to live on one floor.

Of course, we also have to look at the financial implications of each option. We currently have two incomes and share all the expenses, but we would have to figure out what each of us could afford on our own, if we had to. Those calculations have yet to be done.

The takeaway from all this? The best outcome depends on strong advance planning. (For more information, see Appendix D: To Move or Not to Move?, page 229.)

~❧~

*I sometimes wonder how things might have been different for Mom if Dad* had lived longer. Maybe Mom would not have hoarded plastic bags. Maybe Dad would have framed his war medals and discarded his old correspondence instead of stashing it all in locked metal boxes. Mom and Dad might have moved together from my grandfather's house into assisted living, maybe in another province or even another country.

If Mom had understood Gramps's will more clearly she might have moved into long-term care sooner. The will had included a clause that if Mom refused the house, it would be sold, and the proceeds divided among Gramps's four children. Soon after Mom retired and moved in to stay, she asked me if it could be true that she didn't have full ownership of the house. Since she'd already accepted the house, and had paid for its repairs, upgrades, and taxes, I told her I didn't think so, but that she should check with her lawyer. It was another twenty years before she finally consulted Ms. M. and was told the house was clearly hers and she could do what she wanted with it. By that time, Mom had run out of energy for making decisions about selling and moving or renovating and staying. It's both interesting and useless to speculate on what might have been if she'd asked the lawyer earlier. Mom ultimately landed on her feet, just as she always has.

As my mom's experience clearly shows, anyone can become trapped by their responsibilities, surroundings, and possessions. I can already feel it happening to me.

But I promise I will fight back—before it becomes someone else's problem.

# Epilogue

~❧~

My youngest, Marty, called the other day.

"You and Dad are downsizing, right?"

"Yes, we've been trying to cull our possessions for some time," I told him. I didn't add that we were doing it as a favour to our children. No need. Nor did I tell him that I planned to mail him a box of stuff. A big, big box. Maybe two. Or maybe send a truckload.

I knew that he and his siblings had spent the previous weekend together. I envisioned them huddled over pizza and a bottle of wine, talking about Mom and Dad getting old. Marty must have been deputized to initiate the conversation—the same one I'd had with Mom.

"Are you going to sell?"

"Not right yet, but we're thinking about it."

Indeed. A three bedroom, upstairs–downstairs split-entry with 120 acres, a woodlot, flower and vegetable gardens, an orchard, grapes, berry and asparagus patches, a swimming pool, three ponds and a river, a very long driveway, a barn and three other outbuildings, and a sawmill: it's a lot to look after in old age.

"Do it, Mom. Find a smaller place where there is nothing to do but what you guys love to do. Somewhere near the ski hill and the water. Ski and swim and kayak."

"And walk and write and garden and drive around on the quad," I replied. "Far enough away from my neighbours for privacy, but close enough to holler for help. Near the doctor and the stores, but not anywhere in town."

He didn't catch my small, small sarcastic note.

"Yeah, something like that," he agreed enthusiastically.

*The apple doesn't fall far from the tree*, I thought. If you don't learn from history, you're destined to repeat it.

So this is my line in the sand: it's time to get rid of my possessions. It's time to be free of the things that I have to look after—things that I have to maintain or clean with no benefit or reward.

There, I've said it. I am downsizing.

But I am not moving.

Well, not yet.

# Afterword

❦

*A*s we were finishing up the final edits on this book, I was able to visit Mom at The Home. It was meant to be a surprise, but someone had leaked the information to her about my arrival.

I walked in to find her perched on her walker in the lobby, watching the door like a hawk. She didn't recognize me at first, but I was, after all, wearing a mask, as required by COVID-19 regulations.

After I hand-sanitized, signed The Home's visitors' log, and answered questions about my health, Mom galloped me down the hall to her room. She moved swiftly for a 92-year-old pushing a walker.

"Come in, come in," she ordered, closing the door behind me.

Her room looked just like home. A clutter of books filled four of the five chairs, including the two she'd wrestled from the dining room. I sat on the bed, and she took the upholstered rocker. All the other surfaces were covered—buried under magazines, scribbled notes, photos, napkins, placemats, boxes of candies and cookies, clothing, mugs, and bowls containing plants, cutlery, and other items. Over the next couple of days, I discovered she'd collected jam packets from at least two dozen breakfasts. She was unable to identify the origins of most of the new items in her room—from seasonal ornaments to blankets.

She urged me to help her sort her jewellery, photos, greeting cards, and papers. It turned out to be a pleasant trip down memory lane for both of us—albeit a winding one! I was able to tidy the books, fill a garbage bag with junk, take away some items for family members, and consign some tossed-aside clothing to the laundry. I did not find her lost room key, nor could I locate the book I'd created for her with photos of her family members along with their names and addresses.

It was comforting to see her in her element. Every time I'd walked away from Mom over the past decade, though, I'd wondered if it would be the last time I'd see her.

This fond farewell was no different. But at least this time I had no expectation that my tidying efforts would last!

# Continuing Care in the Atlantic Provinces

───❖───

*Housing Nova Scotia, a provincial government agency that works* with regional housing authorities across the province, operates a public housing program that provides apartments to low-income seniors. Rent is adjusted to income. Contact your regional office, listed in the provincial government pages of the phone book under "housing," visit housing.novascotia.ca, or call 211.

The province's Department of Health and Wellness licenses and funds nursing homes. There are two levels of care: continuing care and residential care. Call 211 or the single-entry access number: 1-800-225-7225, or visit novascotia.ca/dhw/ccs/long-term-care. asp. Each applicant is assigned a continuing care coordinator and undergoes an assessment. An applicant deemed not ready to move will not be assessed for placement. Once assessed, that person must accept a space quickly when it is offered. If not, they are removed from the wait-list and cannot reapply for three months.

Applicants placed in a distant community go on a priority list to be transferred a facility closer to their families as soon as a space becomes available.

For placement in a private facility (e.g. The Berkeley, Parkland) individuals can contact the facility directly. No government subsidy is provided, so financial means is an important consideration.

~⋅~

*New Brunswick's Department of Social Development oversees a number* of seniors' programs, including three kinds of adult residential facilities. Licensed, independently owned nursing homes are aimed at medically stable clients in need of nursing care. Special care homes may include sections for people with dementia. Community residences are designed for people who require less care. The department provides funding, manages capital costs, serves in an advisory capacity, and is responsible for determining eligibility of applicants by assessing long-term health and social needs. Each facility manages admissions.

If applicants are able to pay, they must do so, but subsidies are available if needed. A financial assessment is required. An applicant can refuse the first offer of a bed if the proposed placement is not their placement of choice, but any subsequent refusal will result in their name being removed from the waiting list and they will no longer be eligible for admission to any nursing home.

The department also offers at-home supports, fuel supplements, medical transport, supplies and equipment, public housing, rent assistance, and day activities for seniors. Applicants may contact their regional Social Development office at 1-866-444-8388,

call 211 for information, or visit www2.gnb.ca/content/gnb/en/
departments/social_development.html.

~⚬~

*Prince Edward Island's long-term nursing care services are handled by*
Health PEI through a mix of public manors and private nursing
homes, serving people who have physical limitations that hamper
their ability to dress themselves and walk, people with advanced
dementia who may be physically healthy, and younger people who
require nursing care.

Each individual is assessed for the best-suited type of care.
Residents may be subsidized by Social Development and Housing
based on financial need. People in hospital will be moved to the
first available nursing space that matches their needs, which may
not be in their communities. When a placement becomes available
in the home of their choice, they will be moved there. People who
are not in crisis may refuse a placement and still retain their spot
on the waiting list while taking advantage of home care services.
A third refusal results in a re-assessment.

Two housing models are used: traditional large facilities
resembling hospitals, and small house options, which are a series
of smaller "pods" with care targeted toward specific populations.
The province also offers community or residential care facilities:
government-licensed residences that are much like a university
dormitory with medication management. These facilities offer no
nursing services. Subsidies may be available in certain cases. Visit
princeedwardisland.ca/en/information/health-pei/long-term-care
or call (902) 368-5313.

~⋅~

*In Newfoundland and Labrador, people seeking continuing care should* contact their regional health authority to be assessed for their physical, social, and financial needs. Subsidies are available if required, and individuals are matched to a facility that fits their other needs.

Personal care homes are licensed, privately owned-and-operated homes for older adults who need assistance with daily living but who do not need nursing care.

Long-term care is delivered in both long-term care facilities and in some hospitals and health centres. It provides twenty-four-hour nursing care, plus medical rehabilitative, palliative, and other services and programs. Some facilities offer specialized programs and living units for people with special needs such as Alzheimer's disease. For information, visit gov.nl.ca/hcs/long-term-care.

# Creating a Personal Information Kit

⁓⁂⁓

*A* personal information kit can provide your family members with the information they will need if they have to take over the management of your day-to-day activities, either temporarily while you are ill, or permanently if you require long-term care.

Make use of a scribbler, binder, or notebook to keep everything in one place. A binder is simplest to update because pages can easily be added or removed. Whatever you use, clearly mark the outside with your name and a title that makes sense to you. Some options: Personal Matters; My Personal Record Book; Things I Need To Remember In An Emergency; My Book About Me—or whatever you like.

Inside, on the top of the first page, record your name, address, telephone number and other contact information, and your date of birth. It's not a bad idea to put your social insurance number here to make dealing with taxation and other matters easier.

Note the date that you begin preparing this kit. Every time you change some information, cross out the previous date and note the new one.

On the next page, record your health card number and list any medications you take, whether prescription or over-the-counter. Include the dosage. Keep this information up to date!

You may enter the following information in whatever order you choose, but it would be wise to include the categories listed below. (You may think of more.) Each item should be on a separate line, so you can record the appropriate information beside it: service provider, contact information, account number and password, as they apply.

- **Utilities:** power, water, telephone, cable TV, internet, cell-phone.
- **Financial:** bank accounts (automatic withdrawals), investments, credit cards, pensions/benefits, employment income.
- **Insurance:** life, home, auto, disability, health.
- **Subscriptions:** newspapers, magazines, shopping clubs.
- **Organizations and memberships:** religious, lodges, unions, clubs, committees, performance groups, professional organizations.
- **Social media accounts:** Facebook, Twitter, LinkedIn, Instagram, Pinterest.
- **Loyalty Cards:** Air Miles, Plum Points, Canadian Tire, Optimum.
- **Email accounts:** list all your email addresses and passwords.
- **To be notified:** landlord, mortgage company, post office, registry of motor vehicles, Revenue Canada, employer.

- **List location of:** safety deposit box, will, property titles and deeds, car titles, passports, marriage licence/certificate, birth certificate, citizenship papers, military records/discharge papers, bank books, tax records, stocks and bonds, prepaid funeral contracts, proof of intellectual property.
- **Health-care practitioners:** family doctor, medical specialists, pharmacist, physiotherapist, massage therapist, dietician, chiropractor, dentist, psychiatrist/psychologist, optometrist, acupuncturist.

Keep your book in a place you will remember, preferably in a drawer or cupboard where casual visitors don't snoop, but where it can be quickly located in an emergency. Tell a trusted family or friend where you keep it. Make a copy for that person and give it to them for safe-keeping.

*(All information courtesy of Death Matters, Halifax: deathmatters.ca.)*

Appendix C

# *Move Managers and Professional Organizers*

*Move managers and professional organizers are independent entre-*preneurs or larger companies that charge rates that begin at $30/hour and go up from there. Their job is to help people—in some cases, specifically older adults and their families—through the downsizing and relocation process.

An average job can take from seventeen to more than thirty hours, which means that an average move can cost from $500 to more than $1,000. Factors that can affect the price include the size of the house, the number of possessions, the distance of the move, the client's level of readiness, and their willingness to cooperate.

International certification bodies such as the National Association of Senior Move Managers (NASMM) and Professional

Organizers in Canada (POC) ensure their members are properly trained and adhere to codes of safety and professional ethics.

If there are no certified specialists in the region where you live, there is nothing wrong with hiring someone else, as long as they are trustworthy. Ask for recommendations from someone you know.

The best move managers will walk their clients through the decision-making process. You may wish to ask a close friend or family member for help in making those decisions, or you may want to consult someone else you trust to give you honest feedback. Whether you hire a certified professional or an independent contractor, be ready with questions about what to expect, and don't be afraid to state clearly what you want. It's wise to demand a contract that clearly outlines responsibilities and expectations on both sides.

# To Move or Not to Move?

~·~

*T*he best advice for decision-making around where to live as we age is to make your wishes clear while you're healthy and capable, and before you're in crisis—because that's when you can lose control of the decision-making process.

Here are some questions to help you decide whether you'll move or stay in place as you age. Answer honestly!

- Are you able to work in your garden and mow your own lawn? Can you shovel the driveway when it snows? If not, do you have support systems in place to look after these tasks?
- Can you do grocery shopping by yourself? Are you able to cook your own meals?
- Can you do your own laundry and housecleaning?
- Can you manage your own banking and bill-paying?
- Do you feel safe and comfortable living alone in your house?

- Do you need help with dressing, walking, bathing, or grooming?
- Do you need help with stairs? Getting items out of cupboards? Operating appliances?
- Can you go out by yourself (visiting, shopping, to church and other events)?
- Do you have a medical condition that may cause your health to get worse suddenly or within the next twelve months?
- Do you feel like a prisoner in your own house?
- Is your house too big for you? Do you enjoy it as much as you once did?
- Do you have a lot of possessions squirrelled away that you haven't used in years? Does that bother you?
- Can you afford the taxes, insurance, utilities, maintenance, and other expenses?
- Does the house need expensive repairs or updating?
- Is the neighbourhood as enjoyable as it used to be?
- Do you have friends or family living nearby?
- Do you have another important reason for staying?

After answering the above questions, consider which option makes sense to you:

- Staying and reconsidering these questions in a few months.
- Staying and adding services and aids to help you age in place.
- Selling and buying a smaller house or a condo or lease.
- Selling and renting an independent apartment or an apartment with extra services.
- Selling and moving to assisted retirement living.

# Acknowledgements

—◦—

*M*y Mother—*the best. Enough said.*

My brothers, my children, and their families for their hard work, input, cooperation, and support.

To all my extended family and friends—your names have been changed to protect your identities, but you know who you are. Thank you for helping me clean my mother's house; for offering me transportation, a place to lay my head, and financial and other practical advice; for sharing your stories that are so similar to Mom's; and for leaving me alone when I had to write.

To my husband, Martin...oh, never mind. I'll tell you in person.

# Bibliography, Resources, and Further Reading

Bombeck, Erma. *If Life is a Bowl of Cherries, What Am I Doing in the Pits?* Robbinsdale, MN: Fawcett, 1971.

Cilley, Marla. *The Fly Lady.* March 2019. flylady.net.

Death Matters. "Planning Together for End of Life." Accessed March 2020. deathmatters.ca.

Goldberg, Susan. *The Last Chapter: Estate and Legacy Planning for Writers.* Toronto: The Writers' Union of Canada, 2019.

Gray, Douglas and John Budd. *The Canadian Guide to Will and Estate Planning, Fourth Edition.* Toronto: McGraw-Hill Education, 2018.

Kondo, Marie. *The Life-Changing Magic of Tidying Up.* Berkeley: Ten Speed Press, 2014.

Magnusson, Margareta. *The Gentle Art of Swedish Death Cleaning: How to Free Yourself and Your Family from a Lifetime of Clutter.* New York: Scribner, 2018.

National Association of Senior Move Managers. Accessed October 2019. nasmm.org.

Palmer, Brooks. *Clutter Busting: Letting Go of What's Holding You Back*. Novato, CA: New World Library, 2009.

Riley, Sharon J. "The Age of Surrender." *The Walrus*. April 2020.